ENCRYPTION MADE SIMPLE FOR LAWYERS

DAVID G. RIES / SHARON D. NELSON / JOHN W. SIMEK

ABA LAW PRACTICE DIVISION
The Business of Practicing Law

Commitment to Quality: The Law Practice Division is committed to quality in our publications. Our authors are experienced practitioners in their fields. Prior to publication, the contents of all our books are rigorously reviewed by experts to ensure the highest-quality product and presentation. Because we are committed to serving our readers' needs, we welcome your feedback on how we can improve future editions of this book.

Cover design by Kelly Book/ABA Publishing.

Printed in the United States of America.

19 18 17 16 15   5 4 3 2 1

Library of Congress Cataloging-in-Publication Data

Nelson, Sharon, Ries, David & Simek, John authors.

Discounts are available for books ordered in bulk. Special consideration is given to state bars, CLE programs, and other bar-related organizations. Inquire at Book Publishing, American Bar Association, 321 North Clark Street, Chicago, Illinois 60654-7598.

www.ShopABA.org

Dedication

Sharon Nelson and John Simek dedicate this book to our children, Kelly, Sara, Kim, JJ, Jason, and Jamie, and to our grandchildren, Samantha, Lilly, Tyler, Evan, Jordan, Cash, and Parker. Keep those grandchildren coming!

Dave Ries dedicates this book to his wife, Debbie, and his sons and their families, Dave, Jr. and Jenelle (grandchildren, Ellie and Dave III), and Chris and Liz.

Contents

About the Authors

Sharon D. Nelson is the president of Sensei Enterprises, Inc. Ms. Nelson graduated from Georgetown University Law Center in 1978 and has been in private practice ever since. She now focuses exclusively on electronic evidence law.

Ms. Nelson and Mr. Simek are the co-authors of eight editions of *The Solo and Small Firm Legal Technology Guide* (American Bar Association 2008–2015). They are also co-authors of *Locked Down: Information Security for Lawyers* (ABA, 2012). Additionally, Ms. Nelson and Mr. Simek are co-authors of *The Electronic Evidence and Discovery Handbook: Forms, Checklists, and Guidelines* (ABA, 2006). Ms. Nelson is a co-author of *How Good Lawyers Survive Bad Times* (ABA, 2009). Their articles have appeared in numerous national publications, and they frequently lecture throughout the country on digital forensics, information security, and legal technology subjects.

Ms. Nelson is a co-host of Legal Talk Network's "The Digital Edge: Lawyers and Technology and Digital Detectives" podcasts. Ms. Nelson and Mr. Simek have a regular legal tech column called "Hot Buttons" in the ABA Law Practice Division magazine *Law Practice*. Ms. Nelson is a member of the American Bar Association's Cybersecurity Task Force and its Standing Committee on

Technology and Information Systems and is a member of the Editorial Board of *Law Technology News*.

Ms. Nelson is currently the immediate past president of the Virginia State Bar. She is past president of the Fairfax Bar Association, the current president of the Fairfax Law Foundation, past chair of the ABA's TECHSHOW Board, and past chair of the ABA's Law Practice Management Publishing Board. She currently serves as the vice chair of its Education Board. She is a member of the Sedona Conference. She is a graduate of Leadership Fairfax and serves on the Governing Council of the Virginia State Bar as well as on its Executive Committee. She is the former chair of the Virginia State Bar's Unauthorized Practice of Law Committee and serves on both its Standing Committee on Finance and its Special Committee on the Future of Law. She is a member of the ABA, the Virginia Bar, the Virginia Bar Association, the Virginia Trial Lawyers Association, the Virginia Women Lawyers Association, and the Fairfax Bar Association.

Ms. Nelson has served as a Court Appointed Special Advocate for Abused and Neglected Children for the past four years.

John W. Simek is the vice president of Sensei Enterprises, Inc. He is a Certified Information Systems Security Professional (CISSP) and a nationally known testifying expert in the area of digital forensics.

Mr. Simek holds a degree in engineering from the United States Merchant Marine Academy and an MBA in finance from Saint Joseph's University. After forming Sensei, he ended his more than 20-year affiliation with Mobil Oil Corporation, where he served as a senior technologist, troubleshooting and designing Mobil's networks throughout the Western Hemisphere.

In addition to his CISSP certification, Mr. Simek is an EnCase Certified Examiner (EnCE), Certified Handheld Examiner, a

Certified Novell Engineer, Microsoft Certified Professional + Internet, Microsoft Certified Systems Engineer, NT Certified Independent Professional, and a Certified Internetwork Professional. He is also a member of the High Tech Crime Network, the Fairfax Bar Association and the American Bar Association. In addition to co-authoring the books cited in Ms. Nelson's biography, he also serves on the Education and Publishing Boards of the ABA's Law Practice Division and on its governing council. He currently provides information technology support to more than 250 area law firms, legal entities, and corporations. He lectures on legal technology and digital forensics subjects throughout the world.

He is a co-host of Legal Talk Network's "Digital Detectives" podcast.

Mr. Simek also serves as a Court Appointed Special Advocate for Abused and Neglected Children.

David G. Ries is a member in the Pittsburgh office of Clark Hill PLC, where he practices in the areas of environmental, commercial, and technology litigation. He has used computers in his practice since the early 1980s and since then has strongly encouraged attorneys to embrace technology—in secure ways. He served two terms as a member and chair of a hearing committee for the Disciplinary Board of the Supreme Court of Pennsylvania. He received his JD from Boston College Law School in 1974 and his BA from Boston College in 1971.

Mr. Ries has represented clients in a variety of technology litigation matters, including major systems implementation cases, and has advised clients on a number of technology law issues, such as information security and privacy compliance, hardware and software agreements, outsourcing contracts, electronic payments, technology policies, electronic records management, response to computer intrusions, and electronic contracting.

He is chair of the ABA Law Practice Division's Education Board and is a member of the ABA Section of Science and Technology's Information Security Committee and of ILTA's LegalSEC Council. He recently completed two terms as a member of the ABA Law Practice Division Council and served on the ABA TECHSHOW Planning Board from 2005 through 2008.

Mr. Ries frequently speaks on ethics, legal technology, and technology law issues for legal, academic and professional groups including the American Bar Association, the Association of Corporate Counsel, the Energy & Mineral Law Foundation, the Pennsylvania Bar Institute, the Information Systems Security Association and Carnegie Mellon University. He is a co-author of *Locked Down: Information Security for Lawyers* (ABA 2012) and a contributing author to *Information Security and Privacy: A Legal, Business and Technical Handbook,* Second Edition (ABA 2011). He and John Simek wrote "Encryption Made Simple for Lawyers," *GPSolo Magazine* (November/December 2012), and they have presented several webinars on the topic.

Acknowledgments

Thanks go to the reviewers of this book, Tom Mighell, JoAnn Hathaway, Allison Shields and Jeff Flax—their contributions were invaluable—and it takes a lot of time to review a book about encryption. Tom, who serves as the chair of the ABA Law Practice Division Publishing Board, was especially helpful in shepherding this book from the moment we first conceived of it all the way through the publishing process.

We are grateful to have Denise Constantine as our Manager of Book Publishing at the Law Practice Division. She has kept us on track and (almost) on time!

We express our appreciation to Chris Ries, an information security professional who currently focuses on software security (and actually understands the math of encryption). He has provided a lot of helpful input on the technical aspects of this book and shared his security insights with us over the years.

Preface

Like many areas of technology, encryption options continue to evolve and change, sometimes rapidly. For example, during final planning and writing of this book, the following developments occurred:

- The developers of TrueCrypt, a popular open source (and free) encryption program, posted a notice that it would no longer be supported and "is not secure";

- Google and Yahoo announced that they are working on end-to-end encryption for their e-mail;

- Google stated that it will enable encryption by default on Android devices when a user sets up a PIN, password, or swipe pattern, starting with its new operating system, Lollipop;

- Apple (for iOS) and Google (for Android) have announced that they will stop retaining encryption recovery keys for smartphones and tablets, so they will be unable to decrypt devices, even in response to user requests, or to warrants and court orders; and

- Box, a leading cloud file synchronizing and sharing service, reported that it is working on adding end-user-controlled encryption to its business and enterprise services.

We have included in this book encryption solutions about which we have sufficient experience or information to cover them. There will almost certainly be changes in these solutions over time. There are also additional encryption options that we could not cover in a book of this length.

Because of future developments and additional options, it is best to make sure that you have current information when selecting encryption options. Ask someone who stays current on information security or check online resources. For legal technology information, the ABA Law Practice Division (http://www.lawpractice.org) has a number of educational, online, and print resources, including ABA TECH-SHOW, *Law Practice Magazine*, *Law Practice Today* webzine, and the Legal Technology Resource Center. Some additional legal resources are the Law Technology Today blog (http://www.lawtechnology today.org), Digital Edge podcasts (http://legaltalknetwork.com/podcasts/digital-edge), Digital Detectives podcasts (http://legaltalk network.com/podcasts/digital-detectives), Kennedy-Mighell Report podcasts (http://legaltalknetwork.com/podcasts/kennedy-mighell-report), ILTA's LegalSEC initiative (http://connect.iltanet.org/resources/legalsec), and Law Technology News (http://www.law technologynews.com). Some suggested online technology resources include InformationWeek (http://www.informationweek.com), InfoWorld (http://www.infoworld.com), PCWorld (http://www.pcworld.com), and ZDNet (http://www.zdnet.com). For more technical information, SC Magazine (http://www.scmagazine.com) includes reviews and comparisons of information security products and services.

Chapter 1
INTRODUCTION TO THE AMAZING WORLD OF ENCRYPTION

Lawyers tend to cringe when they hear the word "encryption." To most lawyers, encryption is a dark art, full of mathematical jargon and incomprehensible to the average human being.

When South Carolina suffered a major data breach of taxpayer data in 2012, what did Governor Nikki Haley say? "A lot of banks don't encrypt. It's very complicated. It's very cumbersome. There's a lot of numbers involved with it."[1]

Leaving aside the laughable notion that a lot of banks don't encrypt data, the rest of her quote is in keeping with what we hear from lawyers. What we hear always translates into the same thing: Encryption is hard.

We hope to prove to you that encryption isn't hard at all. More than that, we are going to do our level best to persuade you that you may well be required by your ethical duties as a lawyer to encrypt sensitive client data. In the meantime, let's go back in time and show

---

1 "Lies We Tell Our CEOS About Database Security," *Information Week*. http://www.darkreading.com/application-security/database-security/lies-we-tell-our-ceos-about-database-security/d/d-id/1138619. Accessed on October 10, 2014.

you that encryption has been a major player in history—and a staple of childhood.

SECRET DECODER RING

Figure 1.1

So let's make this more fun with some things you can relate to.

Encryption is designed to secure data from prying eyes. It keeps secrets secret. Think about your childhood. Did you play with invisible ink? Did you watch the mailbox for a magic decoder ring like the one author Nelson just got? Perhaps you spoke pig Latin with a sibling so your parents remained clueless about what you were plotting.

You've seen secrets hidden in the movies—remember the World War II Navajo code talkers in *Windtalkers?* Cryptography has been featured in many movies, including the *National Treasure* movies, *Sneakers,* and, perhaps most famously, *The Da Vinci Code.*

See? Cryptography can be fun. Really! So we thought we'd take you back in time to see how dramatically it has impacted our lives.

BASIC TERMS

In the simplest terms, cryptography is the science of secret communication. It involves transmitting and storing data in a form that only the intended recipient can read. Encryption is one form of cryptography.

Encryption is the conversion of data into a form called a ciphertext that cannot be easily understood by unauthorized people. Decryption is the process of converting encrypted data back into its original form (plaintext), so it can be understood.

Read those two definitions a couple of times and presto—you have the essence of what this book is about. Want it simpler still? Here it is in graphic form.

Figure 1.2

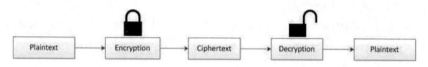

It is a simple representation of a process that can be very complex, but this is the fundamental process that all encryption goes through from start to finish.

GOAL OF ENCRYPTION

The goal of encryption is to make obtaining the information too resource-intensive (time, work, and computing power) to be worthwhile. It is unlikely that there will ever be perfect encryption that can never be broken, particularly over extended periods of time. However, strong encryption, properly implemented, provides very strong protection.

Encryption can protect stored data (on servers, desktops, laptops, tablets, smartphones, portable devices, etc.) and transmitted data (over wired and wireless networks, including e-mail).

HISTORY

In the early days, people carved messages into wood or stone and the recipient had the "key" to know how to translate them. Today, cryptography is far more advanced and is found in streams of binary code that pass over wired networks, wireless networks and Internet communications pathways. Here's a quick trip to see how information was encrypted throughout history.

Hieroglyphics

Cryptography is over 4,000 years old and began in Egypt, where hieroglyphics were used to decorate the tombs to describe the decedent's life stories. They had elements of an alphabet as well as pictographs. They were an art form as well as a kind of language—and only educated Egyptians could read them. As you might imagine, there were not many educated Egyptians at the time.

Figure 1.3

Substitution Ciphers

An early Hebrew cryptographic method "flipped" the alphabet like this.

ABCDEFGHIJKLMNOPQRSTUVWXYZ
ZYXWVUTSRQPONMLKJIHGFEDCBA

In this method, Monday would become OMNWZB.

It seems simplistic to us, but it worked quite well for a time. This is an example of a **substitution cipher** because each character is replaced with another character. This sort of substitution cipher is called a **monoalphabetic substitution cipher** because it uses only one alphabet. A **polyalphabetic substitution** uses multiple alphabets and will be described more fully below.

Scytale Cipher

Around 400 B.C., the Spartans began using a **scytale cipher** (*scytale* means "baton" in Greek). They encrypted information by writing a message on a sheet of papyrus that was wrapped around a wooden rod—this was delivered and wrapped around a different rod by the recipient. The message could only be read if it was wrapped around the correct size wooden rod, which made the letters properly match up. Otherwise, the papyrus simply seemed to contain a batch of random characters.

Figure 1.4

Caesar Cipher

A little later in Rome, Julius Caesar developed what came to be known as (surprise) the **Caesar Cipher.**

Though it would be easily broken by trying all possible combinations, the Roman general used it to good effect in his military career. His cipher utilized a simple shifting of the letters of the alphabet. He shifted each letter by three characters, as seen below:

ABCDEFGHIJKLMNOPQRSTUVWXYZ
DEFGHIJKLMNOPQRSTUVWXYZABC

So long as the key (the three-letter shift) was known to the recipient, any message was easy to decrypt. In a time and place where very few people could read at all, this provided a high degree of protection. In the image below, you can see a variation on Caesar's cipher where the three-letter shift moves to the left as opposed to the right in the example given above.

Figure 1.5

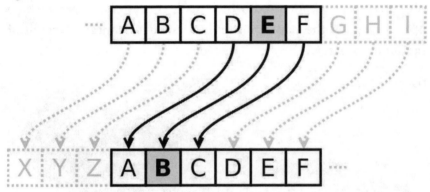

Vigenère Cipher

In the 16th century, Blaise de Vigenère developed a polyalphabetic substitution cipher for Henry VIII. It was actually based on Caesar's Cipher, but the Vigenère Cipher was more complex because it used multiple alphabets. In order to encrypt a message, you needed a keyword and a set of alphabets in a matrix. To encrypt, you took the first letter of the keyword and found it in the column and first letter of plaintext and matched it with the associated row. If the message was longer than the keyword, the keyword would repeat itself. The recipient needed the same matrix and the same key to decrypt the message.

Jefferson Disk

Anyone who has studied the life of Thomas Jefferson appreciates his lively intelligence. He was a prodigious inventor and came up with the **Jefferson Disk** (a cipher wheel) in the late 1790s. Over 150 years later, the U.S. army would use his invention, then called the M-94. Each wheel has a random set of letters. The key was in the arrangement of the 36 disks. The order of the letters is different for each disk and was usually scrambled in some random way. Each disk is marked with a unique number. A hole in the center of the disks allows them to be stacked on an axle. The disks are removable and can be mounted on the axle in any order desired. The order of the disks is the cipher key, and both sender and receiver must arrange the disks in the same predefined order.

Once the disks have been placed on the axle in the agreed order, the sender rotates each disk up and down until a desired message is spelled out in one row. Then the sender can copy down any row of text on the disks other than the one that contains the plaintext message. The recipient simply has to arrange the disks in the agreed-upon order, rotate the disks so they spell out the encrypted message on one row, and then look around the rows until he sees the plaintext message—the one row that isn't total gibberish. Absolutely brilliant for its time!

Figure 1.6

Zimmerman Telegraph

The Zimmerman telegraph was a milestone of cryptography in history. The coded telegraph was sent from Arthur Zimmerman, a German foreign secretary, to a German ambassador in Mexico. It suggested that Mexico declare war against the U.S. for financial benefit and the reclamation of lost territory. The British intercepted the message and decoded it, providing its contents to President Woodrow Wilson. It was a principal factor in getting the United States to enter World War I in 1917.

This was still a substitution cipher but more complex. The letters of the plaintext (message to be put into secret form) were replaced by other letters, numbers, or symbols. In this code system, each letter of the alphabet and each of the numbers from 1 to 9 appeared in the matrix of a grid. Each letter in the grid was replaced by two letters in the coded message. The first letter in the message was from the vertical axis of the grid, and the second letter was from its horizontal axis. Ingenious but, as history proved, crackable.

Figure 1.7

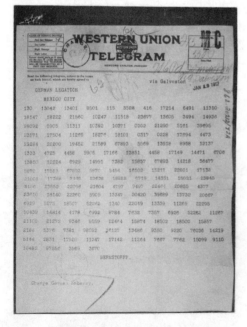

Enigma

Very few readers will be unfamiliar with the German **Enigma** electro-mechanical encryption machine that has been featured in so many movies and TV documentaries. Early versions of this machine were used commercially as early as the 1920s, with additional security enhancements added as time went on.

The Germans adopted Enigma just before the Second World War. No doubt mindful of the Zimmerman incident, their version of Enigma was quite secure. Indeed it remained an "enigma" to Allied intelligence for a long time, until the U.S. Navy captured an Enigma machine and several codebooks on the German U-505 submarine in 1944. Once again, our British friends, this time at the now-famous Bletchley Park, broke the code, undoubtedly bringing the war to an earlier end. The intelligence gleaned from Enigma was called "Ultra." Winston Churchill reportedly told King George VI after the war that "it was thanks to 'Ultra' that we won the war."

Figure 1.8

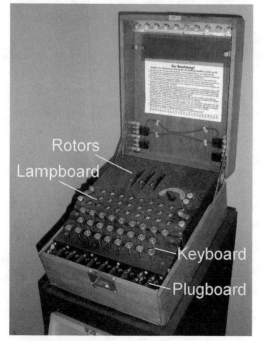

Indian Code Talkers

We made reference earlier to the Navajo code talkers, who helped the U.S. Marine Corps transmit secret messages over telephone and radio during the Second World War. Using the Navajo language, in addition to coding, was much faster than using machines to encrypt and decrypt messages. The use of Indian dialects began in the First World War with the Choctaw code talkers and continued through the Korean War.

Historical Footnotes (just for fun)

Mary Queen of Scots was beheaded in 1587 when she foolishly relied on a substitution cipher for her correspondence with plotters against Queen Elizabeth I. By that time, the existence of substitution ciphers was well known—and those that were not extremely complex were simple to decode.

And a literary sidebar: substitution ciphers appear in Edgar Allen Poe's "The Gold Bug" story and in Sir Arthur Conan Doyle's Sherlock Holmes mystery "Adventure of the Dancing Men." Real life drama and fictional fun—who could ask for more?

Modern Day

We have brought you up to where the rest of this book will go, into the Data Encryption Standard (DES), which was the de facto encryption algorithm for the U.S. government for more than 25 years after being adopted in 1977.

Fortunately, you don't have to understand the math and computer science behind encryption in order to use it. There are now many easy-to-use encryption tools available for end-users. While most attorneys will need help to set up encryption, it's generally not difficult after setup—often automatic or point-and-click.

While we have done our best to make encryption understandable, it does take a certain amount of concentration. So grab a cup of coffee and set aside some "quiet time" to digest how encryption works. Trust us, it has now reached the point where all attorneys should have encryption available for use, where appropriate, to protect client data.

There's an App for That!

For iPad users who want to learn more about the early ciphers in a fun way, there's an app for that. It's the Secret Decoder Ring, available for 99¢ in the App Store.

The app includes electronic versions of the Cipher Disk (like the Secret Decoder Ring) and the Wheel Cipher—both discussed in the preceding chapter—as well as the Quick Brown Fox and the Telephone Cipher.

Chapter 2

ENCRYPTION AND A LAWYER'S DUTY TO SAFEGUARD INFORMATION

Attorneys' use of technology presents special ethics challenges, particularly in the areas of competence and confidentiality. Attorneys also have common law duties to protect client information and may have contractual and regulatory duties. These duties to safeguard information relating to clients are minimum standards with which attorneys are required to comply. Attorneys should aim for even stronger safeguards as a matter of sound professional practice and client service.

Encryption is now a generally accepted practice in information security for protection of confidential data. Attorneys should understand encryption and use it in appropriate situations. All attorneys should use encryption on laptops, smartphones, tablets and portable media that contain information relating to clients. They should also make sure that transmissions over wired and wireless networks are secure, which often requires some form of encryption. In addition, attorneys should have encryption available for e-mail or secure file transfer and use it when appropriate. Although many attorneys will need technical assistance to install and set up encryption, use of encryption after that is generally easy.

ETHICS RULES

The duty of competence (ABA Model Rule 1.1) requires attorneys to know what technology is necessary and how to use it. The duty of confidentiality (ABA Model Rule 1.6) is one of an attorney's most fundamental ethical responsibilities. Together, these rules require attorneys using technology to take competent and reasonable measures to safeguard information relating to clients. This duty extends to all use of technology, including computers, mobile devices, networks, technology outsourcing, and cloud computing, and includes use of encryption where appropriate. This book will help you to decide when encryption may be appropriate.

Model Rule 1.1 covers the general duty of competence. It provides that "[a] lawyer shall provide competent representation to a client." This "requires the legal knowledge, skill, thoroughness and preparation reasonably necessary for the representation." It includes competence in selecting and using technology. It requires attorneys who lack the necessary technical competence for security to consult with qualified people who have the requisite expertise.

Model Rule 1.4, Communications, also applies to attorneys' use of technology. It requires appropriate communications with clients "about the means by which the client's objectives are to be accomplished," including the use of technology. It requires keeping the client informed and, depending on the circumstances, may require obtaining "informed consent." It requires attorneys, where appropriate, to discuss with clients the risks of using technology, including e-mail and electronic communications.

Model Rule 1.6 generally defines the duty of confidentiality. It begins as follows:

> A lawyer shall not reveal information relating to the representation of a client unless the client gives informed consent, the disclosure is impliedly authorized in order to carry out the representation or the disclosure is permitted by paragraph (b)....

Rule 1.6 broadly requires protection of "information relating to the representation of a client;" it is not limited to confidential communications and privileged information. Disclosure of covered information generally requires express or implied client consent (in the absence of special circumstances like misconduct by the client).

The ABA Commission on Ethics 20/20 conducted a review of the ABA Model Rules of Professional Conduct and the U.S. system of lawyer regulation in the context of advances in technology and global legal practice developments. One of its core areas of focus was technology and confidentiality. Its Revised Draft Resolutions in this area were adopted by the ABA at its Annual Meeting in August of 2012.[1]

The amendments include addition of the following highlighted language to the Comment to Model Rule 1.1 Competence:

> [8] To maintain the requisite knowledge and skill, a lawyer should keep abreast of changes in the law and its practice, including the benefits and risks associated with technology . . .

The amendments also added the following new subsection (highlighted) to Model Rule 1.6 Confidentiality of Information:

> (c) A lawyer shall make reasonable efforts to prevent the inadvertent or unauthorized disclosure of, or unauthorized access to, information relating to the representation of a client.

This requirement covers two areas—inadvertent disclosure and unauthorized access. Inadvertent disclosure includes threats like leaving a briefcase, laptop, or smartphone in a taxi or restaurant, sending a confidential e-mail to the wrong recipient, producing privileged documents or data, or exposing confidential metadata. Unauthorized access includes threats like hackers, criminals, malware, and insider threats.

---

1   See, www.americanbar.org/groups/professional_responsibility/aba_commission_on_ethics_20_20.html.

The amendments also include the following changes to Comment [18] to this rule:

Acting Competently to Preserve Confidentiality

[18] Paragraph (c) requires a A lawyer must to act competently to safeguard information relating to the representation of a client against unauthorized access by third parties and against inadvertent or unauthorized disclosure by the lawyer or other persons or entities who are participating in the representation of the client or who are subject to the lawyer's supervision or monitoring. See Rules 1.1, 5.1 and 5.3. The unauthorized access to, or the inadvertent or unauthorized disclosure of, confidential information does not constitute a violation of paragraph (c) if the lawyer has made reasonable efforts to prevent the access or disclosure. Factors to be considered in determining the reasonableness of the lawyer's efforts include the sensitivity of the information, the likelihood of disclosure if additional safeguards are not employed, the cost of employing additional safeguards, the difficulty of implementing the safeguards, and the extent to which the safeguards adversely affect the lawyer's ability to represent clients (e.g., by making a device or important piece of software excessively difficult to use). A client may require the lawyer to implement special security measures not required by this Rule or may give informed consent to forego security measures that would otherwise be required by this Rule. Whether a lawyer may be required to take additional steps to safeguard a client's information in order to comply with other law, such as state and federal laws that govern data privacy or that impose notification requirements upon the loss of, or unauthorized access to, electronic information, is beyond the scope of these Rules.

Significantly, these revisions are clarifications rather than substantive changes. They add additional detail that is consistent with the then existing rules and comments, ethics opinions, and generally accepted information security principles.[2]

---

2   "This duty is already described in several existing Comments, but the Commission concluded that, in light of the pervasive use of technology to store and transmit confidential client information, this existing obligation should be stated explicitly in the black letter of Model Rule 1.6." ABA Commission on Ethics 20/20, *Report to Resolution 105A Revised*, Introduction (2012).

Model Rule 5.3 (Responsibilities Regarding Nonlawyer Assistants) was amended to expand its scope. "Assistants" was expanded to "Assistance," extending its coverage to all levels of staff and outsourced services ranging from copying services to outsourced legal services. This requires attorneys to employ reasonable safeguards, like due diligence, contractual requirements, supervision, and monitoring, to ensure that non-lawyers inside and outside a law firm provide services in compliance with an attorney's duty of confidentiality.

ETHICS OPINIONS

A number of state ethics opinions have addressed professional responsibility issues related to security in attorneys' use of various technologies. Consistent with the Ethics 20/20 amendments, they generally require competent and reasonable safeguards. It is important for attorneys to consult the rules, comments, and ethics opinions in the relevant jurisdiction(s).

An early example is State Bar of Arizona, Opinion No. 05-04 (July 2005) (Formal Opinion of the Committee on the Rules of Professional Conduct). It requires "competent and reasonable steps to assure that the client's confidences are not disclosed to third parties through theft or inadvertence" and "competent and reasonable measures to assure that the client's electronic information is not lost or destroyed." It further explains that "an attorney must either have the competence to evaluate the nature of the potential threat to the client's electronic files and to evaluate and deploy appropriate computer hardware and software to accomplish that end, or if the attorney lacks or cannot reasonably obtain that competence, to retain an expert consultant who does have such competence."

Additional examples include New Jersey Advisory Committee on Professional Ethics, Opinion 701, "Electronic Storage and Access of Client Files" (April 2006), State Bar of Arizona, Opinion No. 09-04 (December 2009): "Confidentiality; Maintaining Client Files;

Electronic Storage; Internet" (Formal Opinion of the Committee on the Rules of Professional Conduct); State Bar of California, Standing Committee on Professional Responsibility and Conduct, Formal Opinion No. 2010-179; and New York State Bar Association Ethics Opinion 1019, "Confidentiality; Remote Access to Firm's Electronic Files," (August 2014).

Significantly, California Formal Opinion No. 2010-179 advises attorneys that they must consider security **before** using a particular technology in the course of representing a client. It notes that attorneys "must take appropriate steps to evaluate," among other considerations, "the level of security attendant to the use of that technology, including whether reasonable precautions may be taken when using the technology to increase the level of security." The opinion covers use of a firm-issued laptop and use of public and home wireless networks.

New York Opinion 1019 cautions attorneys to analyze necessary precautions in the context of current risks:

> Cyber-security issues have continued to be a major concern for lawyers, as cyber-criminals have begun to target lawyers to access client information, including trade secrets, business plans and personal data. Lawyers can no longer assume that their document systems are of no interest to cyber-crooks. That is particularly true where there is outside access to the internal system by third parties, including law firm employees working at other firm offices, at home or when traveling, or clients who have been given access to the firm's document system.

The opinion leaves it up to attorneys and law firms to determine the specific precautions that are necessary:

> Because of the fact-specific and evolving nature of both technology and cyber risks, we cannot recommend particular steps that would constitute reasonable precautions to prevent confidential information from coming into the hands of unintended recipients, including the degree of password protection to ensure that persons who access the system are

authorized, the degree of security of the devices that firm lawyers use to gain access, whether encryption is required, and the security measures the firm must use to determine whether there has been any unauthorized access to client confidential information.

It requires attorneys to either make a determination that the selected precautions provide reasonable protection, in light of the risks, or to obtain informed consent from clients after explaining the risks.

There are now multiple ethics opinions on attorneys' use of cloud computing services like online file storage and software as a service (SaaS).[3] For example, New York Bar Association Committee on Professional Ethics Opinion 842, "Using an outside online storage provider to store client confidential information" (September 2010), consistent with the general requirements of the ethics opinions above, concludes:

> A lawyer may use an online data storage system to store and back up client confidential information provided that the lawyer takes reasonable care to ensure that confidentiality is maintained in a manner consistent with the lawyer's obligations under Rule 1.6. A lawyer using an online storage provider should take reasonable care to protect confidential information, and should exercise reasonable care to prevent others whose services are utilized by the lawyer from disclosing or using confidential information of a client. In addition, the lawyer should stay abreast of technological advances to ensure that the storage system remains sufficiently advanced to protect the client's information, and the lawyer should monitor the changing law of privilege to ensure that storing information in the "cloud" will not waive or jeopardize any privilege protecting the information.

Additional examples of opinions covering cloud services are Pennsylvania Bar Association, Committee on Legal Ethics and Professional Responsibility, Formal Opinion 2011-200, "Ethical

---

3   The ABA Legal Technology Resource Center has published a summary with links, "Cloud Ethics Opinions Around the U.S.," *available at* www.americanbar.org/groups/departments_offices/legal_technology_resources/resources/charts_fyis/cloud-ethics-chart.html.

Obligations for Attorneys Using Cloud Computing/Software as a Service While Fulfilling the Duties of Confidentiality and Preservation of Client Property" (November 2011) and North Carolina State Bar 2011 Formal Ethics Opinion 6, "Subscribing to Software as a Service While Fulfilling the Duties of Confidentiality and Preservation of Client Property" (January 2012).

The key professional responsibility requirements from these various opinions on attorneys' use of technology are **competent and reasonable measures to safeguard client data**, including an understanding of limitations in attorneys' competence, obtaining appropriate assistance, continuing security awareness, appropriate supervision, and ongoing review as technology, threats, and available security evolve.

ETHICS RULES—ELECTRONIC COMMUNICATIONS

E-mail and electronic communications have become everyday communications forms for attorneys and other professionals. They are fast, convenient, and inexpensive, but also present serious risks. It is important for attorneys to understand and address these risks.

In addition to adding the requirement of reasonable safeguards to protect confidentiality, the Ethics 2000 revisions to the Model Rules, over ten years ago, also added Comment 17 [now 19] to Rule 1.6. This comment requires reasonable precautions to safeguard and preserve confidential information during electronic transmission. This Comment, as amended in accordance with the Ethics 20/20 recommendations (highlighted), provides:

> [19] When transmitting a communication that includes information relating to the representation of a client, the lawyer must take reasonable precautions to prevent the information from coming into the hands of unintended recipients. This duty, however, does not require that the lawyer use special security measures if the method of communication affords a reasonable expectation of privacy. Special

circumstances, however, may warrant special precautions. Factors to be considered in determining the reasonableness of the lawyer's expectation of confidentiality include the sensitivity of the information and the extent to which the privacy of the communication is protected by law or by a confidentiality agreement. A client may require the lawyer to implement special security measures not required by this Rule or may give informed consent to the use of a means of communication that would otherwise be prohibited by this Rule. Whether a lawyer may be required to take additional steps in order to comply with other law, such as state and federal laws that govern data privacy, is beyond the scope of these Rules.

This Comment requires attorneys to take "reasonable precautions" to protect the confidentiality of electronic communications. Its language about "special security measures" has often been viewed by attorneys as providing that they never need to use encryption. While it does state that "special security measures" are not generally required, it contains qualifications and notes that "special circumstances" may warrant "special precautions." It includes the important qualification—**"if the method of communication affords a reasonable expectation of privacy."** As discussed below, there are questions about whether Internet e-mail affords a reasonable expectation of privacy.

ETHICS OPINIONS—ELECTRONIC COMMUNICATIONS

An ABA ethics opinion in 1999 and several state ethics opinions have concluded that special security measures, like encryption, are not routinely required for confidential attorney e-mail.[4] However,

---

4   E.g., ABA Formal Op. No. 99-413, *Protecting the Confidentiality of Unencrypted E-Mail* (March 10, 1999) ("based upon current technology and law as we are informed of it . . . a lawyer sending confidential client information by unencrypted e-mail does not violate Model Rule 1.6(a) . . ." " . . . this opinion does not, however, diminish a lawyer's obligation to consider with her client the sensitivity of the communication, the costs of its disclosure, and the relative security of the contemplated medium of communication. Particularly strong protective measures are warranted to guard against the disclosure of highly sensitive matters.") and District

these opinions should be carefully reviewed because, like Comment 19, they contain qualifications that limit their general conclusions.

For example, New York Bar Association Committee on Professional Ethics Opinion 709 "Use of Internet to advertise and to conduct law practice focusing on trademarks; use of Internet e-mail; use of trade names" (September 1998) concludes:

> We therefore conclude that lawyers may in ordinary circumstances utilize unencrypted Internet e-mail to transmit confidential information without breaching their duties of confidentiality . . . to their clients, as the technology is in use today. Despite this general conclusion, lawyers must always act reasonably in choosing to use e-mail for confidential communications, as with any other means of communication. Thus, in circumstances in which a lawyer is on notice for a specific reason that a particular e-mail transmission is at heightened risk of interception, or where the confidential information at issue is of such an extraordinarily sensitive nature that it is reasonable to use only a means of communication that is completely under the lawyer's control, the lawyer must select a more secure means of communication than unencrypted Internet e-mail.
>
> A lawyer who uses Internet e-mail must also stay abreast of this evolving technology to assess any changes in the likelihood of interception as well as the availability of improved technologies that may reduce such risks at reasonable cost. It is also sensible for lawyers to discuss with clients the risks inherent in the use of Internet e-mail, and lawyers should abide by the clients' wishes as to its use.

As discussed below, security professionals have questioned the security of unencrypted e-mail for years—comparing it to a postcard that can be easily read. Consistent with these questions about the security of e-mail, some ethics opinions express a stronger view that encryption may be required. For example, New Jersey Opinion 701 (April 2006), discussed above, notes at the end: "where a document

---

of Columbia Bar Op. 281, "Transmission of Confidential Information by Electronic Mail," (February 1998), ("In most circumstances, transmission of confidential information by unencrypted electronic mail does not per se violate the confidentiality rules of the legal profession. However, individual circumstances may require greater means of security.").

is transmitted to [the attorney] . . . by email over the Internet, the lawyer should password a confidential document (as is now possible in all common electronic formats, including PDF), since it is not possible to secure the Internet itself against third party access."[5]

California Formal Opinion No. 2010-179, also discussed above, notes that "encrypting email may be a reasonable step for an attorney in an effort to ensure the confidentiality of such communications remain so when circumstances call for it, particularly if the information at issue is highly sensitive and the use of encryption is not onerous."

An Iowa opinion on cloud computing suggests the following as one of a series of questions that attorneys should ask when determining appropriate protection: "Recognizing that some data will require a higher degree of protection than others, will I have the ability to encrypt certain data using higher level encryption tools of my choosing?" Iowa Ethics Opinion 11-01.

The recent Pennsylvania ethics opinion on cloud computing concludes that "attorneys may use email but must, under appropriate circumstances, take additional precautions to assure client confidentiality." It discusses encryption as an additional precaution that may be required when using services like web mail. Pennsylvania Formal Opinion 2011-200.

In addition to complying with any legal requirements that apply, the most prudent approach to the ethical duty of protecting confidentiality is to have an express understanding with clients (preferably in an engagement letter or other writing) about the nature of communications that will be (and will not be) sent electronically and whether or not encryption and other security measures will be utilized.

---

5   As discussed in Chapter 11, file password protection in some software, like current versions of Microsoft Office, Adobe Acrobat, and WinZip, uses encryption to protect security. It is generally easier to use than encryption of the e-mail message and attachments. However, the protection can be limited by use of weak passwords that are easy to break or "crack."

It has now reached the point where attorneys should have encryption available for use in appropriate circumstances. If you doubt this, read the next chapter carefully and we'll tell you why.

COMMON LAW DUTIES

Along with these ethical duties, there are also parallel common law duties defined by case law in the various states. The Restatement (Third) of the Law Governing Lawyers (2000) summarizes this area of the law. See Section 16(2) on competence and diligence, Section 16(3) on complying with obligations concerning client's confidences, and Chapter 5, "Confidential Client Information." Breach of these duties can result in a malpractice action.

There are also instances when lawyers have contractual duties to protect client data. This is particularly the case for clients in regulated industries, such as health care and financial services, that have regulatory requirements to protect privacy and security. Clients are recognizing that law firms may be the weak links in protecting their confidential information and are increasingly requiring specified safeguards, providing questionnaires about a law firm's security, and even requiring security audits.

LAWS AND REGULATIONS COVERING PERSONAL INFORMATION

In addition to the ethical and common law duties to protect client information, various state and federal statutes and regulations require protection of defined categories of personal information. Some of these apply to lawyers who possess any specified personal information about their employees, clients, clients' employees or customers, opposing parties and their employees, or even witnesses.

At least 12 states now have general information security laws that require reasonable measures to protect defined categories of personal information (Arkansas, California, Connecticut, Illinois, Maryland, Massachusetts, Nevada, New Jersey, Oregon, Rhode Island, Texas, and Utah). While the scope of coverage, the specificity of the requirements, and the definitions vary among these laws, "personal information" is usually defined to include general or specific facts about an identifiable individual. The exceptions tend to be information that is presumed public and does not have to be protected (e.g., a business address).

The most comprehensive law of this type to date is a Massachusetts law,[6] which applies to "persons who own, license, store or maintain personal information about a resident of the Commonwealth of Massachusetts." Covered "personal information" includes Social Security numbers, driver's license numbers, state-issued identification card numbers, financial account numbers, and credit card numbers. With its broad coverage of "persons," this law is likely to be applied to persons nationwide, including attorneys and law firms, when they have sufficient contacts with Massachusetts to satisfy personal jurisdiction requirements. It requires covered persons to "develop, implement, and maintain a comprehensive information security program that is written in one or more readily accessible parts and contains administrative, technical, and physical safeguards."

The implementing regulation[7] for the Massachusetts law became effective in 2010. In addition to requiring a risk assessment, the regulation contains detailed requirements for the information security program and detailed computer system security requirements. The security requirements include:

- encryption of all transmitted records and files containing personal information that will travel across public networks,

---

6 Mass. Gen. Laws, Ch. 93H.

7 201 C.M.R. 17.00.

and encryption of all data containing personal information to be transmitted wirelessly; and

- encryption of all personal information stored on laptops or other portable devices.

Additional system security requirements in the Massachusetts regulation are secure user authentication, secure access control, reasonable monitoring to detect unauthorized access, reasonably up-to-date firewall protection, reasonably up-to-date security software (including current patches and virus definitions), and education and training of employees.

Nevada also has laws that require "reasonable security measures" and encryption,[8] although they are much less detailed than the Massachusetts law.

The legal obligations don't stop, however, at protecting the confidentiality of information. Forty-seven states and the District of Columbia and the Virgin Islands have laws that require notification concerning data breaches (all but Mississippi, New Mexico, and South Dakota). While there are differences in their scope and requirements, they generally require entities that own, license, or possess defined categories of personally identifiable information about consumers to notify affected consumers if there is a breach. Like the reasonable security laws, many of these laws apply to covered information "about" residents of the state. Some require notice to a state agency in addition to notice to consumers. Most of these laws have encryption safe harbors, which provide that notice is not required if the data is encrypted and the decryption key has not been compromised.

At the federal level, an attorney who receives protected individually identifiable health information (PHI) from a covered entity under the Health Insurance Portability and Accountability Act (HIPAA) will be a "business associate" and be required to comply

---

8   Nev. Rev. Stat. 603A.210 and 597.970.

with the HIPAA security requirements. The 2009 Healthcare Information Technology and Clinical Health (HITECH) Act enhanced HIPAA security requirements, extended them directly to business associates, and added a new breach notification requirement. Encryption is included as an "addressable" requirement, which means that it or an alternative must be implemented or a written explanation provided to explain why it is not needed. See 45 CFR Parts 160 and 164.

Note too that encryption is already required for federal agencies that have information about individuals on laptops and portable media.[9] This requirement was adopted after a high-profile data breach in which a laptop and external drive were stolen from the car of an employee of the Department of Veterans Affairs, exposing personal information of approximately 27 million veterans.

The Federal Trade Commission has brought a number of enforcement actions against businesses based on allegations that they failed to take reasonable measures to safeguard the privacy and security of personal information about consumers. In over half of them, settlements required the businesses to employ additional safeguards, including encryption of personal information in transmission and storage.[10]

As encryption becomes a legal requirement in areas like these, it is likely to become the standard of what is reasonable for lawyers.

SUMMARY OF DUTIES

The ethics rules and common law duties require attorneys to take **competent and reasonable measures to safeguard client data,**

---

9   Office of Management and Budget Memorandum M-06-16 (June 23, 2006) ("Encrypt all data on mobile computers/devices which carry agency data unless the data is determined to be non-sensitive . . .")

10 Patricia Bailin, *Study: What FTC Enforcement Actions Teach Us About Features of Reasonable Privacy and Data Security Practices*, The Privacy Advisor (Sept. 19, 2014), https:privacy association.org.

including an understanding of limitations in attorneys' competence, obtaining appropriate assistance, continuing security awareness, appropriate supervision, and ongoing review as technology, threats, and available security evolve. **These ethical and common law duties, as well as any applicable contractual and regulatory duties, are minimum standards of conduct. Attorneys should aim for even stronger safeguards as a matter of sound professional practice and client service.** While the risks of disciplinary proceedings, malpractice claims, and regulatory actions arising from security breaches are real, the greatest risks are often dissatisfied clients (or former clients) and harm to professional reputation.

INFORMATION SECURITY BASICS

Information security is a process to protect the confidentiality, integrity, and availability of information. Security starts with a risk assessment to identify anticipated threats to the information assets, including an inventory of information assets to determine what needs to be protected. The next step is development and implementation of a comprehensive information security program to employ reasonable physical, administrative, and technical safeguards to protect against identified risks. This is the most difficult part of the process. It must address people, policies and procedures, and technology and include assignment of responsibility, training, ongoing security awareness, monitoring for compliance, and periodic review and updating.

The requirement for lawyers is *reasonable* security, not absolute security. New Jersey Ethics Opinion 701 states "'[r]easonable care,' however, does not mean that the lawyer absolutely and strictly guarantees that the information will be utterly invulnerable against all unauthorized access. Such a guarantee is impossible . . ." Recognizing this concept, the Ethics 20/20 amendments to the Comment to Rule 1.6 include ". . . [t]he unauthorized access to, or the inadvertent or unauthorized disclosure of, confidential information does not constitute a violation of paragraph (c) if the lawyer has made reasonable efforts to prevent the access or disclosure."

ENCRYPTION AND REASONABLE SAFEGUARDS

The greatest challenge for lawyers in establishing information security programs is deciding what security measures are necessary and then implementing them. Determining what constitute "competent and reasonable measures" can be difficult. The Ethics 20/20 amendments provide some high-level guidance in Comment 18 to Rule 1.6. As discussed above, the following factors are applied for determining reasonable and competent safeguards:

> Factors to be considered in determining the reasonableness of the lawyer's efforts include the sensitivity of the information, the likelihood of disclosure if additional safeguards are not employed, the cost of employing additional safeguards, the difficulty of implementing the safeguards, and the extent to which the safeguards adversely affect the lawyer's ability to represent clients (e.g., by making a device or important piece of software excessively difficult to use).

Weighing of these factors supports the use of encryption by attorneys, where appropriate, particularly for highly sensitive data. There has been growing recognition of the risk of exposure of unencrypted data, particularly during transmission and on mobile and portable devices. At the same time, there has been increasing availability of inexpensive and easy-to-use encryption solutions.

Mobile Devices

Protection of laptops, smartphones, tablets, and other mobile devices presents a good example of application of the requirement of "reasonable efforts" to a specific category of technology. Mobile devices present a great security risk because they can be easily lost or stolen.

The *Verizon 2014 Data Breach Investigation Report* (covering 2013) explains the risk and a solution to it—encryption—this way:[11]

> ### PHYSICAL THEFT AND LOSS
>
> ### RECOMMENDED CONTROLS
>
> The primary root cause of incidents in this pattern is carelessness of one degree or another. Accidents happen. People lose stuff. People steal stuff. And that's never going to change. But there are a few things you can do to mitigate that risk.
>
> *Encrypt devices.*
>
> ***
>
> Considering the high frequency of lost assets, **encryption is as close to a no-brainer solution as it gets** for this incident pattern. Sure, the asset is still missing, but at least it will save a lot of worry, embarrassment, and potential lawsuits by simply being able to say the information within it was protected. . . . (Emphasis added.)

It's not just Verizon. This view is widely held by information security professionals and government agencies. While attorneys and law firms have to determine what is reasonable in their circumstances, this raises the question, does failure to use encryption for mobile devices—a no-brainer solution—comply with the duty to employ reasonable safeguards?

E-mail

E-mail is another good example for application of this analysis. There are serious questions about the confidentiality of Internet e-mail. Respected security professionals for years have compared e-mail to postcards or postcards written in pencil.[12] A June 2014

---

11 www.verizonenterprise.com/DBIR/2014/.

12 E.g., B. Schneier, *E-Mail Security: How to Keep Your Electronic Messages Private*, (John Wiley & Sons, Inc. 1995) p. 3; B. Schneier, *Secrets & Lies: Digital Security in a Networked Work*, (John Wiley & Sons, Inc. 2000) p. 200 ("The common metaphor for Internet e-mail is postcards: Anyone—letter carriers, mail sorters, nosy delivery truck drivers—who can touch the postcard can read what's on the back."); and Larry Rogers, *Email—A Postcard Written in Pencil*, Special Report, (Software Engineering Institute, Carnegie Mellon University 2001).

post by Google on the *Google Official Blog*[13] and a July 2014 *New York Times* article[14] use the same analogy—comparing unencrypted e-mails to postcards. Encryption is being increasingly required in areas like banking and health care. Recent laws in Nevada[15] and Massachusetts[16] (which apply to attorneys as well as others) require defined personal information to be encrypted when it is electronically transmitted. As the use of encryption grows in areas like these, it will become difficult for attorneys to demonstrate that confidential client data needs lesser protection.

Comment [19] to Model 1.6 states that a lawyer is not required to "use special security measures if the method of communication affords a reasonable expectation of privacy." The references above suggest that unencrypted e-mail—like a postcard—does not. The Comment also lists "the extent to which the privacy of the communication is protected by law" as a factor to be considered. The federal Electronic Communications Privacy Act[17] makes unauthorized interception of electronic communications a crime. Some observers have expressed the view that this should be determinative and attorneys are not required to use encryption. The better view is to treat legal protection as only one of the factors to be considered. As discussed above, some of the newer ethics opinions conclude that encryption may be a reasonable measure that should be used, particularly for highly sensitive information.

---

13 "Transparency Report: Protecting Emails as They Travel Across the Web," *Google Official Blog* (June 3, 2014) ("... we send important messages in sealed envelopes, rather than on postcards. ... Email works in a similar way. Emails that are encrypted as they're routed from sender to receiver are like sealed envelopes, and less vulnerable to snooping—whether by bad actors or through government surveillance—than postcards.") http://googleblog.blogspot.com/2014/06/transparency-report-protecting-emails.html.

14 Molly Wood, "Easier Ways to Protect Email From Unwanted Prying Eyes," *New York Times* (July 16, 2014) ("Security experts say email is a lot more like a postcard than a letter inside an envelope, and almost anyone can read it while the note is in transit. The government can probably read your email, as can hackers and your employer.") www.nytimes.com/2014/07/17/technology/personaltech/ways-to-protect-your-email-after-you-send-it.html?r=0.

15 Nev. Rev. Stat. 603A.010, *et seq.*

16 Mass. Gen. Laws, Ch. 93H, regulations at 201 C.M.R. 17.00.

17 18 U.S.C. § 2510, *et seq.*

CONCLUSION

Attorneys have ethical and common law obligations to take competent and reasonable measures to safeguard information relating to clients. They also often have contractual and regulatory requirements. Encryption is now a generally accepted practice in information security for protection of confidential data and is required by law for some data. In order to comply with their various duties and to engage in sound professional conduct, attorneys should understand encryption and have it available for use in appropriate situations.

Chapter 3

WHY IS ENCRYPTION SO IMPORTANT FOR LAWYERS?

As we discussed in the previous chapter, attorneys have ethical and common law duties to protect client information and may have contractual and regulatory duties. Some contracts and laws require encryption. Ethics opinions are moving to recognizing encryption as a safeguard that may be required. In addition, common law duties are likely to consider encryption as a requirement as it is increasingly required by laws and more widely adopted in other businesses and professions. These duties to safeguard information relating to clients are minimum standards with which attorneys are required to comply. Failing to meet them is unethical or unlawful conduct.

Attorneys should aim for even stronger safeguards as a matter of sound professional practice and client service. Excellence and client service are growing themes in law practice management and in legal marketing. Attorneys and law firms should strive for excellence and quality client service in safeguarding information relating to clients.

So here's why you should use encryption now. If you want to fully comply with the letter and the spirit of all of these duties, encryption is truly the only way that you can reasonably protect sensitive client data.

Put simply, encryption works. As cybersecurity expert Bruce Schneier has famously said, encryption "drives the NSA batty."[1] That's because strong encryption can stop, or at least challenge, even the NSA. Strong encryption provides a formidable defense against more common security threats.

DATA BREACHES HAVE PROLIFERATED!

It is almost impossible to listen to the news on television without hearing of a data breach. 2014 has us reeling—after the massive Target breach of 2013, we had P.F. Chang's, Sally Beauty Supply, ACME Markets, Michaels Stores, Goodwill Industries, Jimmy John's, Neiman Marcus, Home Depot (56 million credit cards hacked), JPMorgan Chase (76 household and seven million small businesses involved)[2]—and as we write, Kmart and Dairy Queen have recently announced breaches.

Now we hear you saying—"but these aren't law firms." There are a couple of responses to that. One is that we could list a number of law firms that have been breached, some of which are a matter of public record and include law firms both large and small. We don't see the point of embarrassing them by naming them but the information is easily available to anyone who cares to research it.

Confidential data in computers and information systems, including those used by attorneys and law firms, faces greater security threats today than ever before. They take a variety of forms, ranging from e-mail phishing scams and social engineering attacks (humans convincing other humans to do something that allows access to data such as giving up their login credentials) to sophisticated technical exploits resulting in long-term intrusions into law firm networks.

---

1   "Schneier: NSA Snooping Tactics Will Be Copied by Criminals in 3 to 5 Years," *The Register.* https://www.schneier.com/news/archives/2014/02/schneier_nsa_snoopin.html. Accessed on October 11, 2014.

2   "10 Biggest Data Breaches of 2014 (So Far)." *Credit Union Times.* http://www.cutimes.com/2014/10/06/10-biggest-data-breaches-of-2014-so-far. Accessed October 14, 2014.

For years, there were (and still are) numerous law firm incidents of dishonest insiders and lost or stolen laptops and portable media. Over the last several years, there have also been increasing reports in the popular, legal, and security media of successful attacks on attorneys and law firms. Law enforcement agencies and security consultants have been reporting that they are seeing hundreds of law firms being targeted by hackers. They have noted that law firms are often viewed as the "soft underbellies" of confidential data about their clients because law firms frequently have weaker security than their clients. Mandiant, a leading cybersecurity firm now owned by FireEye, noted in 2012 that 80 law firms were breached in 2011.[3]

Security threats to law firms have continued to grow. In February 2013, the special agent in charge of the FBI's cyber operations in New York City gave a keynote presentation on law firm security threats at a legal technology conference. In an article reporting on it, she is quoted as stating:[4]

> "We have hundreds of law firms that we see increasingly being targeted by hackers. . . . We all understand that the cyberthreat is our next great challenge. Cyber intrusions are all over the place, they're dangerous, and they're much more sophisticated" than they were just a few years ago.

Later in 2013, Mandiant's general counsel and vice president of legal affairs explained the extent of current security threats to law firms this way:[5]

> Law firms need to understand that they're being targeted by the best, most advanced attackers out there. . . . These attackers will use every

---

3   Michael A. Riley and Sophia Pearson, "China-Based Hackers Target Law Firms to Get Secret Deal Data," *Bloomberg News* (January 31, 2012), http://www.bloomberg.com/news/2012-01-31/china-based-hackers-target-law-firms.html. Accessed October 30, 2014.

4   Evan Koblenz, "LegalTech Day Three: FBI Security Expert Urges Law Firm Caution," *Law Technology News* (February 1, 2013), www.lawtechnologynews.com/id=1202586539710?slreturn=20140103164728.

5   Joe Dysart, "New hacker technology threatens lawyers' mobile devices," *ABA Journal Law News Now* (September 1, 2103). www.abajournal.com/magazine/article/new_hacker_technology_threatens_lawyers_mobile_devices.

resource at their disposal to compromise law firms because they can, if successful, steal the intellectual property and corporate secrets of not just a single company but of the hundreds or thousands of companies that the targeted law firm represents. Law firms are, in that sense, "one-stop shops" for attackers.

Why don't you hear about more law firm breaches? There are many reasons. Typically, they don't make the headlines like high-profile retail and bank breaches. Some law firms may disclose the breach only to clients so it may not become public. In those cases, both the clients and the law firms may prefer to avoid publicity.

Sometimes, mobile devices that are stolen are encrypted, so there is no requirement to disclose. And sometimes, when unencrypted devices are stolen, lawyers may not appreciate that this triggers a duty to disclose a breach.

Unfortunately, there are some cases in which law firms choose not to disclose a breach to clients. From our private discussions with attorneys from firms who have been breached, the decision was made not to disclose the breach to clients for fear of reputational damage—and probably the exodus of clients as well.

Consider this snippet from a conversation that two partners from a large law firm in New York that suffered a data breach had with Alan Paller, the Director of Research from the SANS Institute.

> Alan: So I have a question. What are you planning to tell your clients?
>
> Attorneys: Are you crazy? Can you think of a better way to destroy their trust in us than letting them know we had lost every document they gave us under (attorney-client) privilege?[6]

Not letting clients know seems to us to be an ethical breach.

---

6   Forbes, "Conversations On Cybersecurity: The Trouble With China, Part 1," Updated January 31, 2012, http://www.forbes.com/sites/ciocentral/2012/01/31/conversations-on-cybersecurity-the-trouble-with-china-part-1/. Accessed October 14, 2014.

THE PAINFUL COSTS OF DATA BREACHES

Make no mistake about it—data breaches are costly. According to the 2014 breach report from the Ponemon Institute, the total average cost is $3.5 million per breach (the large players skew the numbers upwards, as you might imagine). This represents a 15 percent increase over the 2013 numbers.[7]

Figure 3.1

This is where the Benjamin Franklin's adage, "An ounce of prevention is worth a pound of cure"[8] comes dramatically into play. What happens when you have a data breach? Do you have any idea how much it is likely to cost your firm?

Let's start with lost time while you and your partners are dealing with the crisis. That time will mount up fast as you discharge the following duties—which should, of course, be detailed in your Incident Response Plan. You need to call law enforcement in. A crime has been committed. In most cases, law firms call the FBI, if, indeed, the FBI is not the entity that comes to the firm to advise it that it has been breached—and this is a common occurrence.

You need to call a data breach lawyer—unless you have one in house and most law firms do not. You're going to need help complying with all federal and state laws and regulations. What kind of personally identifiable data do you have? HIPAA data? Sarbanes-Oxley data? You may find yourself subject to more laws and regulations than you knew existed.

---

7   "Ponemon Institute Releases 2014 Cost of Data Breach: Global Analysis." Ponemon Institute. http://www.ponemon.org/blog/ponemon-institute-releases-2014-cost-of-data-breach-global-analysis. Accessed October 14, 2014.

8   The Quotable Franklin. http://www.ushistory.org/franklin/quotable/singlehtml.htm. Accessed October 14, 2014.

You may have to pay for notification of your clients and possibly offer them credit card monitoring at your expense, depending on how well you encrypt payment data.

Calling in digital forensics investigators is critical—and they are not cheap. You want folks who hold serious credentials as they investigate the source breach and the vulnerability(ies) that caused it. This can take a long time—and oh, don't forget the money you are going to have to spend to remediate the cause of the breach.

Do you now need a public relations firm to help handle the post-breach nightmare of publicity?

How are you going to persuade your clients that you have addressed the security issues? Are you now going to have to assure clients that you will submit to an annual information security audit? That is very likely—and can be a fairly large annual expense to absorb.

A footnote here: Have you looked at your insurance policies to see if any of this would be covered? The likelihood is that you have not. We ask this question of audiences all the time when we lecture and we rarely see more than a single hand go up. Sometimes, not one hand goes up.

Generally, insurance policies will pay if your computers are stolen for the fair market or replacement value of the computers, depending on your policy. But will they pay for all the expenses we have enumerated above? No. Most insurers have a separate cyberinsurance rider, which is both very expensive and hard to understand, even for lawyers. If you haven't taken a look at your policies recently, this might be an excellent time.

THE ETHICAL DUTIES OF LAWYERS ARE CHANGING WITH TECHNOLOGY

With increasing concerns about data security, the American Bar Association in 2012 revised its ethics rules to explicitly require lawyers to "make reasonable efforts" to protect confidential information from unauthorized disclosure to outsiders. When these amendments were being finalized, a *Wall Street Journal* article observed:[9]

> Think knowing how to draft a contract, file a motion on time and keep your mouth shut fulfills your lawyerly obligations of competence and confidentiality?
>
> Not these days. Cyberattacks against law firms are on the rise, and that means attorneys who want to protect their clients' secrets are having to reboot their skills for the digital age.

And then came Edward Snowden's leaks in 2013. Snowden's revelations have shaken many lawyers, especially since they revealed that the NSA was receiving attorney-client communications from a U.S. law firm representing an Indonesian client in trade talks. Note that we said trade talks, which appear to have nothing at all to do with terrorism. This is where lawyers really need to worry—if much of NSA gathering has to do with economic and political information gathering, many law firms may be targeted.

On February 15, 2014, the *New York Times* reported, in a headline that sent shock waves through the legal sector, "Spying by N.S.A. Ally Entangled U.S. Law Firm."[10]

A top-secret document obtained by Edward Snowden showed that an American law firm was monitored while representing Indonesia in trade disputes with the United States. Attorney-client communications were almost certainly obtained by the Australian version of the NSA, the Australian Signals Directorate, which notified the NSA that it was conducting surveillance of the talks,

---

9   Jennifer Smith, "Client Secrets at Risk as Hackers Target Law Firms," *Wall Street Journal* (June 25, 2012).

10   "Spying by N.S.A. Ally Entangled U.S. Law Firm," *The New York Times*. http://www.nytimes.com/2014/02/16/us/eavesdropping-ensnared-american-law-firm.html?_r=0. Accessed on October 12, 2014.

including communications between Indonesian officials and the American law firm, and offered to share the information.

On behalf of the Australians, the liaison officials asked the NSA general counsel's office for guidance about the spying. The bulletin notes only that the counsel's office "provided clear guidance" and that the Australian agency "has been able to continue to cover the talks, providing highly useful intelligence for interested US customers."

The ABA was already concerned as noted by the passage of the 2012 Resolution, described above. But after the first Snowden revelations, it passed another resolution in 2013. Resolution 118 read as follows:

> RESOLVED, That the American Bar Association condemns unauthorized, illegal governmental, organizational and individual intrusions into the computer systems and networks utilized by lawyers and law firms;
>
> FURTHER RESOLVED, That the American Bar Association urges federal, state, local, territorial, and tribal governmental bodies to examine, and if necessary, amend or supplement, existing laws to promote deterrence and provide appropriate sanctions for unauthorized, illegal intrusions into the computer networks utilized by lawyers and law firms;
>
> FURTHER RESOLVED, That the American Bar Association urges the United States government to work with other nations and organizations in both the public and private sectors to develop legal mechanisms, norms and policies to deter, prevent, and punish unauthorized, illegal intrusions into the computer systems and networks utilized by lawyers and law firms;
>
> FURTHER RESOLVED, That while the American Bar Association supports governmental actions, policies, practices and procedures to combat these unauthorized, illegal intrusions into the computer systems and networks utilized by lawyers and law firms, the ABA opposes governmental measures that would have the effect of eroding the attorney-client privilege, the work product doctrine, the confidential lawyer-client relationship, or traditional state court and bar regulation and oversight of lawyers and the legal profession; and

> FURTHER RESOLVED, That the American Bar Association urges lawyers and law firms to review and comply with the provisions relating to the safeguarding of confidential client information and keeping clients reasonably informed that are set forth in the Model Rules of Professional Conduct, as amended in August 2012 and as adopted in the jurisdictions applicable to their practice, and also comply with other applicable state and federal laws and court rules relating to data privacy and cybersecurity.

The interesting part of this resolution was how it was changed. Originally, it only referenced the intrusions by foreign governments. After the NSA revelations, the word "foreign" was eliminated.

Once the ABA had information from press reports that attorney-client communications had been the target of surveillance, ABA President James Silkenat wrote a letter to the then director of the NSA, General Keith Alexander and General Counsel Rajesh De on February 20, 2014. The letter essentially asked what policies and practices the NSA had to protect privileged information received or intercepted and whether those policies and practices were complied with.[11]

The March 10 answer from General Alexander said that the NSA was "firmly committed to the rule of law and the bedrock principle of attorney-client privilege."[12] Notable was the frequent use of the word "appropriate." The ABA was assured that the NSA would provide "appropriate protection" for privileged documents and institute measure as appropriate.

All of these, of course, would be reviewed by the FISA Court, whose proceedings are secret.

---

11 American Bar Association. http://www.americanbar.org/content/dam/aba/uncategorized/GAO/2014feb20_privilegedinformation_l.authcheckdam.pdf. Accessed October 14, 2014.

12 American Bar Association. http://www.americanbar.org/content/dam/aba/images/abanews/nsa_response_03102014.pdf. Accessed October 14, 2014.

Yet another ABA resolution passed in August 2014. Resolution 109 said,

> RESOLVED, That the American Bar Association encourages private and public sector organizations to develop, implement, and maintain an appropriate cybersecurity program that complies with applicable ethical and legal obligations, and is tailored to the nature and scope of the organization, and the data and systems to be protected.

You might be forgiven for saying "huh?" Clearly, this is an aspirational resolution. It was originally longer and referenced national and international standards. There was a hue and cry over asking too much of small firms (amidst other objections) and the final version was agreeable to all because it refers to the "nature and scope of the organization."

WHO IS THE REAL THREAT?

The greatest threat to solo and small firms is certainly cybercriminals. The 2014 Verizon data breach report examined data breaches in 2013. It found that 60 percent of breaches were the work of cybercriminals, 25 percent the work of state-sponsored hackers, and 8 percent the work of insiders.[13] It is startling how quickly the numbers of state-sponsored hackers have risen, but it would be foolish to focus solely on them (and their advanced attacks) when cybercriminals are still the primary threat.

The report also identifies physical loss and theft of portable devices as a major threat, and notes that encryption is a "no-brainer" solution to protect against it.

No matter who is responsible, most hackers can be confounded by strong encryption. You will hear that a lot in this book—because this is the message we bring to lawyers—encryption is your first and best line of defense.

---

13 The report may be downloaded at http://www.verizonenterprise.com/DBIR/2014/. Accessed October 14, 2014.

ENCRYPTION IS PART OF THE SECURITY PROCESS

As we explained in the previous chapter, information security is a process to protect the confidentiality, integrity, and availability of information. Security starts with a risk assessment to identify anticipated threats to the information assets, including an inventory of information assets to determine what needs to be protected. The next step is development and implementation of a comprehensive information security program to employ reasonable physical, administrative, and technical safeguards to protect against identified risks. It must address people, policies and procedures, and technology and include policies, assignment of responsibility, training, ongoing security awareness, monitoring for compliance, and periodic review and updating. Encryption should be viewed by attorneys in the context of this overall security process.

Figure 3.2

Photograph by Rama, Wikimedia Commons license, Cc-by-sa-2.0-fr

As security guru Bruce Schneier says, it is not enough to think encryption is the full answer. Heed these words: "The mantra of any good security engineer is: **'Security is a not a product, but a process.'** It's more than designing strong cryptography into a system; it's designing the entire system such that all security measures, including cryptography, work together."

Figure 3.3

And are you training your employees on security at least every year? Not doing so presents a serious danger. As Mr. Schneier also says, "The user's going to pick dancing pigs over security every time."[14]

---

14 Native Intelligence, Inc. http://www.nativeintelligence.com/ni-free/itsec-quips.asp. Accessed October 14, 2014.

So remember that encryption, policies, training, constant security education, etc.—it's all a process—and it's never over because the bad guys are always moving forward and we must match them move for move.

Figure 3.4

Photo by Laura Poitras/Praxis Films
Licensed under the Creative Commons
Attribution 3.0 Unported License

We have a strong advocate for encryption in Edward Snowden.

Snowden believes that we should put our faith in technology, not politicians. He has said, "We have the means and we have the technology to end mass surveillance without any legislative action at all, without any policy changes." The answer, he says, is robust encryption. "By basically adopting changes like making encryption a universal standard—where all communications are encrypted by default—we can end mass surveillance not just in the United States but around the world."[15]

What about the argument heard from so many lawyers that encryption is too expensive?

Figure 3.5

Herewith, another famous quote from Benjamin Franklin which provides an answer to that question. "Beware of little expenses. A small leak will sink a great ship."[16]

---

15 "The Most Wanted Man in the World," *Wired,* http://www.wired.com/2014/08/edward-snowden/ #ch-2. Accessed on October 11, 2014.

16 BrainyQuote. http://www.brainyquote.com/quotes/quotes/b/benjaminfr135836.html. Accessed October 12, 2014.

Well said, Mr. Franklin.

And what about those who claim it is too hard? That argument holds no water either.

As the previous chapter noted, you don't **need** to understand encryption. You just need to understand how to use it. Remember learning how to use e-mail—and then, how to send an attachment? Or learning the process of creating, modifying, and saving a Word document? The process of encrypting is no more difficult than that.

To put it simply, lawyers are running out of excuses for their failure to implement encryption. In a breach-a-day world, encryption is the reasonable measure lawyers should take to protect their client data.

According to Mandiant's 2013 Threat Report, 7 percent of the industries being targeted by advanced attackers were legal and consulting services.[17] A lot of law firms are included in that 7 percent—the FBI has stated that it's in the hundreds.

Figure 3.6

So encrypt your data and your devices—you'll sleep better at night. And as Bruce Schneier says on his famous T-shirt, "Trust the Math."

---

17 The 2013 Threat Report from Mandiant can be downloaded at https://dl.mandiant.com/EE/ library/M-Trends_2013.pdf?elq=555c1ff329004eb49ffbeba4cd04df70&elqCampaignId=. Accessed October 14, 2014.

Chapter 4

THE BASICS OF ENCRYPTION TECHNOLOGY (SOME TECH STUFF YOU *MAY* WANT TO KNOW)

This chapter picks up from the description of encryption in the Introduction, including the Data Encryption Standard (DES) algorithm. It covers some weighty (and to some scary) topics, like algorithms, keys and key pairs, symmetric and asymmetric encryption, digital certificates, and hashes. For those who chose law school instead of engineering school because they didn't want to deal with this kind of stuff, we have good news. You don't have to understand encryption technology—even the basics.

If you're comfortable working with technology, like installing and updating software, you can probably review the following chapters and install and use most encryption options yourself. If not, you can get someone who is qualified to help in selecting an encryption solution and setting it up for you. From there, it's generally easy—often automatic or point and click. This chapter explores the basics of encryption for those who want a general (but certainly not a technical[1]) understanding.

Techspeak Warning

This chapter digresses from our "made simple" approach and explores some basic technical aspects of encryption. If you're not interested in this tech stuff, you can skip this chapter and move on to the next one. You'll be able to use the various encryption options that we discuss in the rest of the book, maybe with some help in selecting them and setting them up. Or, if you take the plunge into this chapter and then decide that you've read enough, you can stop, move on to the rest of the book, and use the encryption tools. This chapter covers information that is helpful for those who want to understand it, but not necessary for using encryption.

THE ENCRYPTION PROCESS

As explained in the Introduction:

Encryption is the conversion of data from a readable form, called plaintext, into a form called ciphertext that cannot be easily understood by unauthorized people.

Decryption is the process of converting encrypted data back into its original form (plaintext), so it can be understood.

Encryption can protect stored data (on servers, desktops, laptops, tablets, smartphones, portable devices, etc.) and transmitted data (over wired and wireless networks, including the Internet and e-mail). We explore the details of encrypting both kinds of data in the remaining chapters.

---

1 For those who really want a technical understanding of encryption, we suggest college or grad school level study of math and cryptography or intensive self-study. Bruce Schneier, the true master of cryptography, has written or coauthored the classics for this level of study: Niels Ferguson, Bruce Schneier, and Tadayoshi Kohno, *Cryptography Engineering* (Wiley 2010), Niels Ferguson and Bruce Schneier, *Practical Cryptography* (Wiley 2003), and Bruce Schneier, *Applied Cryptography: Protocols, Algorithms, and Source Code in C* (Wiley, 2nd. Ed. 1996). He maintains a website, *Schneier on Security* (https://www.schneier.com) and publishes a monthly newsletter, *Crypto-Gram* (https://www.schneier.com/crypto-gram.html).

Figure 4.1 The Encryption and Decryption Process

Encryption uses a mathematical formula to convert the readable plaintext into unreadable ciphertext. The mathematical formula is an **algorithm** (called a cipher). Decryption is the reverse process that uses the same algorithm to transform the unreadable ciphertext back to readable plaintext. The algorithms are built into encryption programs—users don't have to deal with them when they are using encryption.

The following is an example of unreadable ciphertext:

Figure 4.2 Example of Encrypted Data—Ciphertext

```
•êµ¡Mg

Y=t,V˙.ý»)'§Â˜C§ƒ^qÏt!"ÿÑHÿ®Çç~¡ôî=ÉÏDZ=[ì»
G"®?êâ!9D˙G© H₅QåÄX¢âÔ£™˙æ,WÜE `Å5¡I–yî2²—
Æ6.¢BÜ!XsaAÎÀx°\1¢W$ÍqïL+€q°Ù†¡,.H,°ƒjØÉDh·½ý¡7bŠ;ñçtó  Êñn;ù#¿ÎfúóAOÑIKÜ£‡Šê—
VWêµð

ð
°.È ˌþ˝ïv†AKù–*ˌA®ˌtDÅ[êTvÇ2ûÅiâf ê³×n5• 9Ÿ+☐œřŠúPéá  €ó¿Oqx{

g lEuœ\ß_˜˙o°|⁹⁄₄]¹⁄₄˙³⁄₄(N  ÿÜÕÔ£ˌÿµÞ£>C»rG¹+6L6–
>1{‡☐˙yc˝¥icxŽUÞ+¥ÉÎ§*ï¾4  ˌn…Ç←~ʻZái$µ4ÿ¢F>Xj–ì»QÕ§*Ñnoâ¶˝õ+ÿz:thþ¦ç˙q×Š¼Êµ¾˜
YÔP]ﬁ;  —6¥wW(c±vƒÕ
Sˌ¿  FÑ,ÉA<BìjõCÔxŽ<9h—Nvn˙à0sÙ¾"  ™#oŒâˌßÞÙ°µÞ°WÅŸ-
ôõÛtÀ•Áfãò"}☐Æñw  ŸzcýŽa2
üŸÎ0UÕ¾ât,üiàOu•Ç  ¡ù)  0ÎÎ#_Y£Åè??7Ü62˝®A!oò {+fÚq™ᵖB,ê›

/ë=ß¸õÓ%%¥ÿÊ˜[  ²>×R},<W{–
ŽžÙŸˌ˜>µúäÙ"JE  zÕ}…vKŸjN  ☐§6eƒ%☐â(9îùEÎ W×Ä DÎÞAt £Ÿù•¦»^Ò—¥J‰oü¹ß-
H,2\>  ,h

3áoﬀᴶ²²?9w]á☐‰  }<8½ÊOy6,àe>  Z)Ð˙ìgtOÎ»Šó˙;¾

°5ývÞi_ùù1â÷CÝ[õ¼ᴵĵiq‡ç#Ùnjà¹@Š–|@˝Ù-
<☐Mä?çÎýAC<&YJˣx  éˉ|á×ˌôMv¶  É®Éœ¶|˝úg°Lƒâ±awïigF&Å(
```

Encryption keys are used to implement encryption for a specific user or users. A key generator that works with the selected encryption algorithm is used to generate a unique key or keys for the user(s). A key is just a line or set of data that is used with the algorithm to encrypt and decrypt the data. Protection is provided by use of the algorithm with the unique key or keys.

The process is called **secret key** or **symmetric key encryption** where the same key is used with an algorithm to both encrypt and decrypt the data. With secret key encryption, it is critical to protect the security of the key because it can be used by anyone with access to it to decrypt the data.

Where a **key pair** is used, one to encrypt the data and a second one to decrypt the data, the process is called **asymmetric encryption**. For this kind of encryption, a key generator is used to generate a unique key pair, one for encryption (a public key) and the other for decryption (a private key). With key pairs, it is critical to protect the private decryption key since anyone with access to it can decrypt the data.

Here is an example of a secret key obtained from a key generator for an algorithm called the Advanced Encryption Standard-256 (AES-256) algorithm (discussed in the next section). The same key is used to both encrypt and decrypt the data.

Figure 4.3 Example AES-256 Key

```
+30NbBBMy7+1BumpfmN8QPHrwQr36/vBvaFLgQM561Q=
```

Let's look at a simple example of its application. A short line of readable plaintext, "This is an encryption demo," becomes unreadable ciphertext when this key is used with the algorithm in an encryption program.

Figure 4.4 Simple Example of Encryption

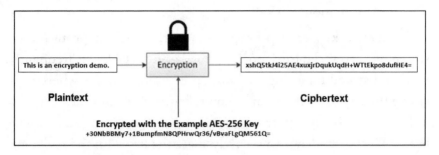

The same key must be used with the algorithm in an encryption program to convert the ciphertext back to readable plaintext.

Figure 4.5 Simple Example of Decryption

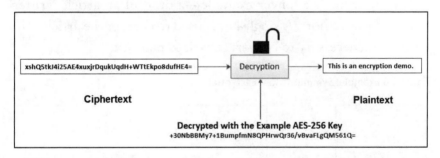

This example was prepared as a short demonstration by generating the key with an online key generator.[2] The key was then used on a website on which users can plug their AES keys into a program to encrypt or decrypt data.[3] Readers who want to explore encryption in more detail can use these kinds of online resources. (*Note:* Using a symmetric [secret] key on a public website would be a poor security practice because it would expose the key that is used for both

---

2   http://www.digitalsanctuary.com/aes-key-generator.php.

3   http://aesencryption.net/.

encryption and decryption. This was a demo key generated and used for this demonstration.)

Symmetric key encryption is frequently used to protect data stored on servers, laptops, portable media, etc. The key is frequently used and stored on a single computer or mobile device where providing the key to someone at a remote location is not necessary. It is difficult to use symmetric key encryption for communications because it is a challenge to securely share the key with the recipient.

Fortunately, users don't have to deal with keys during everyday use. When they log on with the correct password or passphrase, the program automatically accesses the key to decrypt the data. When they log off or shut down, the data is automatically encrypted.

The following is a longer example—a draft of an article written by two of the authors. A single key is used to encrypt the article. The same key is necessary to convert it back to plaintext.

Figure 4.6 Example: Symmetric Key Encryption

Readable Plaintext — Encryption — Unreadable Ciphertext — Decryption — Readable Plaintext — Same Key

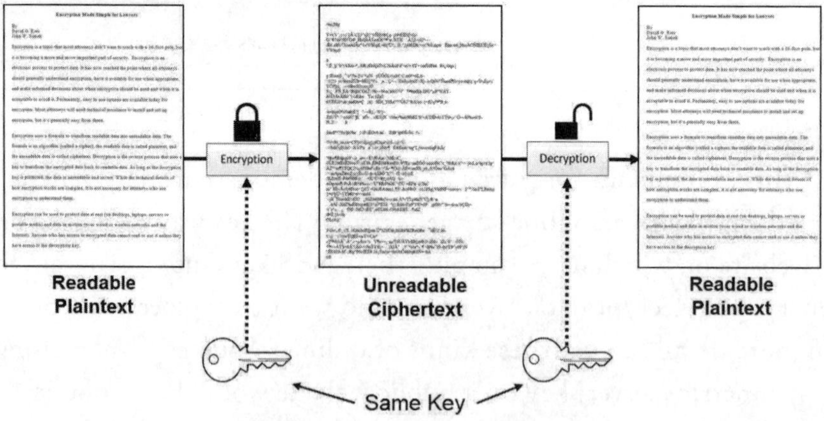

Here's an enlarged view of the plaintext and ciphertext:

Figure 4.7 Enlarged Example: Symmetric Key Encryption

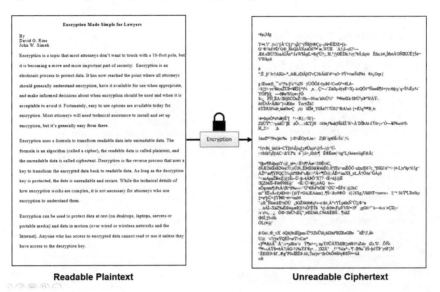

We'll now turn to asymmetric encryption that uses a key pair instead of a single key—one key (a public key) is used to encrypt the data and a second one (a private key) is used to decrypt the data. Key pairs are frequently used for encrypted communications. The sender uses the recipient's public encryption key to encrypt the communication. The public key cannot decrypt it; only the decryption key can do that. The recipient uses the decryption (private key) to decrypt the data.

A common implementation of asymmetric encryption is Public Key Infrastructure (PKI) for electronic communications like e-mail. The public encryption key can be shared with anyone or everyone because it can only be used to encrypt data. There are even public online directories for public keys. The decryption (private) key must be carefully protected and never shared because it is used to decrypt the data.

The following are examples of a public and a private key used with PGP (Pretty Good Privacy), an asymmetric encryption program commonly used for e-mail.

Figure 4.8 Example PGP Key Pair

```
-----BEGIN PGP PUBLIC KEY BLOCK-----
Version: BCPG C# v1.6.1.0

mQENBFQwSmMBCACUzZSg0wVU1lEdmNNUEqG2aGWE6fei5VN2IuEA5FzJIO69JZ7v
VSfMrnw0kA41Bi7EtaJPKS/UIZPEWdcPccIWuiqk8EMEOmq5u1s0AwLeQDsrysXx
BfcXRaxzQrsqLIKq0tpoAwlCNlaMKSuX321EJCNcLbzfdVHmLbgePARXpFmTX4Lf
VkqFX9YBRvbBb2MU9XoB7I0TRQLET1Hc9rbz9UIdLCTK8wt6bGDhpje/N6+szwN0
LQWOllsc+/GcjvJxyA7TKOs0kHltygGRhXI21pfLeHfl3OOf9Cjxd+vzqBp6RXPE
qHKCHqlvX9ucNqiWKcGwcaKgNZgj5z58ssAxABEBAAG0AIkBHAQQAQIABgUCVDBK
XwAKCRABekQY/hFjjbQOB/0R49hb8+AQ1S3BJOnuhLDGwjIW3HXQDPmABO7VudRN
uNmBh8RCwS+mjdpYGmh1ZCvOnHWqleQDX7HTGfpjI+B1Sa7JRPzmsmgRQzi1k6vH
hVotUFaVDmjsQJ//NUbQTH5qmfFZfYtsi6TU79gX+hJiDXRXPT9JVZzcvpaB2hYo
qQ+U6GZTFV1WFRoXpt/BvES7/NzJPUP9HWhXTVyzJEqUBIQ4+Jd4N2hVYTWs8cSg
K2DIra5zyMDrZAimde1d58iEu6s1dds9DHp+V6piWxhsCkjU0LJmRmOHYXnsTCXM
5H/BYicIwJbFHJfr17EC5swDYqKB+/SFefgknveiBc3O
=bVNd
-----END PGP PUBLIC KEY BLOCK-----
```

Example PGP Public Key

```
-----BEGIN PGP PRIVATE KEY BLOCK-----
Version: BCPG C# v1.6.1.0

lQOsBFQwSmMBCACUzZSg0wVU1lEdmNNUEqG2aGWE6fei5VN2IuEA5FzJIO69JZ7v
VSfMrnw0kA41Bi7EtaJPKS/UIZPEWdcPccIWuiqk8EMEOmq5u1s0AwLeQDsrysXx
BfcXRaxzQrsqLIKq0tpoAwlCNlaMKSuX321EJCNcLbzfdVHmLbgePARXpFmTX4Lf
VkqFX9YBRvbBb2MU9XoB7I0TRQLET1Hc9rbz9UIdLCTK8wt6bGDhpje/N6+szwN0
LQWOllsc+/GcjvJxyA7TKOs0kHltygGRhXI21pfLeHfl3OOf9Cjxd+vzqBp6RXPE
qHKCHqlvX9ucNqiWKcGwcaKgNZgj5z58ssAxABEBAAH/AwMCP3SM+rSPjNgYbDn
Na6pQIJVDjRsBB1/+zIpmRSsNjfYlQdWiLmYRpjRebAtmcg2uEON/87VkG5W0A7Z
uWvo4j6wSBhL61JODf1EuFNOEcC7s2DiTWPYmBufgfBrJUhgVHMfX74buUWqRqxx
tMa/K8Qk3oOddljWtrZtxNIm0T1GhegLTIMnQpm2iWmH1f8CPjezUg+ej/oCnKvU
80hbX0rhuAlTyNyh326HMQXAQHOjElA/gRLhGmB4LajyzShT0PTE5ZN7SMZpDYWQ
3kLhWuu1qF1EFsx0rH/tS5M4vxsMX6/P39UcJK/Qo2J5n//27iVIaXTFJAD1foya
v7PhyP17krLaTSunDab5ZFVXLZCN41diZN1ikrA+MlIMiMsZa8yDYGhTfYbsY1An
cxLAJIP1dE1nv+LaMFac9aXsWzOT5aH0wSNvnJHlHrP6JMwZUTIKoy1h64zC4T6d
Eiv2p63pVIWpN8ue8FWf8dgqiJSmlo40a6OWJTsjwxv7CagwhtyIB906yfuBi7nD
iZnhGVJUarSVHrC//UFmYRAJY7yNrKVIxjAC277rzlCnEQPIcEqID6Xkkb/4VSwn
+jqrla720Ydyh31IK1b4pSITfVv1MkFzTM1ULhjedt+n06q1OObVAFA2ZJe+0pSH
3LuLEa5AnH5ySRE0B5wOOldJAHRLCXFhE1M4rGVyxEZzJxkNLovST1ZlDoyruow
uBVYpfTbklwla5cfxo1H3Vz6t55vPwTHCP9PVa8V+49iWA5OhgFgCcQl7FbnNFGk
hSGpbi+e6p2h2MDZXwc38Svh0uEGEr3ctA3wOGlb0bOwXZRxpewM0kV0I8R7139h
yeU3ghIZQ0b2AS4co7hcZc8TkxOG/TZi4V1GewDAirQAiQEcBBABAgAGBQJUMEpj
AAoJEAF6RBj+EWONtA4H/RHj2Fvz4BDVLcEk6e6EsMbCMhbcddAM+YAE7tW51E24
2YGHxELBL6aN21gaaHVkR86cdaqV5ANfsdMZ+mMj4HVJrslE/OayaBFDOLWTq8eF
Wi1QVpUOaOxAn/81RtBMfmqZ8V19i2yLpNTv2Bf6EmINdFc9P01VnNy+loHaFiip
D5ToZlMVXVYVGhem38G8RLv83Mk9Q/OdaFdNXLMkSpQEhDj4l3g3aFVhNazxxKBd
kMitrnPIwOtkCKZ17V3nyIS7qyV12z0Men5XqmJbGGwKSNTQsmZGY4dheexMJczk
f8FiJwjAlsUcl+vXsQLmzANiooH79IV5+CSe96IFzc4=
=2n4C
-----END PGP PRIVATE KEY BLOCK-----
```

Example PGP Private Key

Graphically, the process works this way:

Figure 4.9 Example of Public Key Encryption

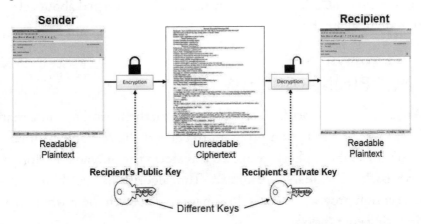

Encryption keys vary in length, from relatively short ones, like the AES example above, to much longer keys, like the PGP example. Key lengths are described in bits (a digital unit, each a 1 or a 0).[4] AES-256 uses a 256-bit key. Secret key encryption can be very secure with keys of this size. The longer the key size with the same encryption algorithm, the stronger it is. So properly implemented AES-256 is stronger than AES-128, which uses a key that is half the length. Key size varies with different algorithms. As the PGP example illustrates, much longer keys are used for both the private key and the public key in asymmetric encryption.

This is an overview of how the encryption process works to protect data. **If a current, generally accepted encryption algorithm (cipher) is used, it is properly implemented, and the decryption key is protected, encryption provides very strong protection of data—making it practically impossible to decrypt the data.** Generally accepted encryption algorithms have often provided strong protection for years before weaknesses in them have been found or

---

4   A very astute observer would notice that the AES-256 key in Figure 4.3 is displayed in letters, numbers, and symbols, rather than 1s and 0s. It has been translated from 1s and 0s by a computer process called encoding.

sufficient computing power has become available to break them. Attorneys adopting commonly used encryption solutions like the ones in this book do not generally have to be concerned about selection of an algorithm.

ENCRYPTION ALGORITHMS

An encryption algorithm (or cipher) is a mathematical formula that is used in an encryption program to convert the readable plaintext into unreadable ciphertext and to transform the unreadable ciphertext back to readable plaintext. The algorithms are built into encryption program—users don't have to deal with them when they are using encryption.

We will briefly review some common algorithms and show that current algorithms can provide very strong protection for data over extended periods of time, often decades. As discussed in the Introduction, the Data Encryption Standard (DES) algorithm was the approved encryption algorithm for the U.S. government for more than 25 years after being adopted in 1977. It is a symmetric algorithm that is now considered to be insecure for many applications. DES evolved into 3DES, which basically repeats the encryption process multiple times, making it stronger. DES was replaced in 2001 with the Advanced Encryption Standard (AES) as a symmetric algorithm for federal agencies and is currently used worldwide. One of the factors that determines the strength of an encryption algorithm is the length of the key. AES uses key sizes of 128, 192, or 256 bits. The example above is a 256-bit key.

For asymmetric encryption, the RSA algorithm (cryptosystem) is commonly used. It was publicly announced in 1977, but remained classified until 1997. It is regularly used for Public Key Infrastructure (PKI) using a matched public key and private key. A new generation of public key cryptography called Elliptic Curve Cryptography (ECC) has been gaining popularity in recent years. It is reported to be significantly more secure than earlier public key cryptography systems.

AUTHENTICATION, INTEGRITY, AND NONREPUDIATION

In addition to protecting the confidentiality of data, cryptography can also establish authentication of the sender (or author), demonstrate the integrity of the message (or document), and establish that the sender sent it (or author wrote it) (called nonrepudiation). This can be done with **digital signatures**. Calculating and attaching a digital signature to a message (or document) is commonly referred to as **signing** the message (or document).

While the following description of digital signing has a number of steps at each end, it is usually point and click or automatic, once set up.

In order to create a **digital signature** for a message, the sender first uses a hash function, which computes a unique hash value for the message (like a digital fingerprint). Next, the sender encrypts the hash value with his or her private key. A recipient can then use the sender's public key to decrypt the hash value. The recipient can then calculate the hash value of the message to make sure that it matches the decrypted value from the sender. This process ensures that the message was not altered after being signed by the sender (which demonstrates integrity), and also guarantees that the sender possesses the private key associated with the public key that was used to verify the signature (which verifies the identity of the sender).

Figure 4.10 Example of Signing an E-mail

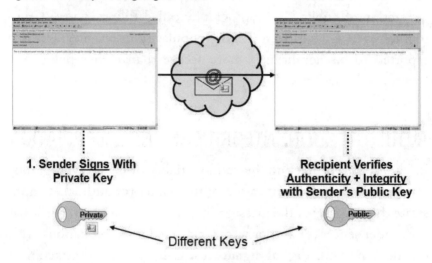

To both (1) establish authenticity, integrity, and nonrepudiation and (2) protect confidentiality, using Public Key Infrastructure, a two-step process is necessary—both signing and encrypting. In order to sign and encrypt an e-mail, the sender first signs the message with his or her private key, then encrypts the message with the recipient's public key. The recipient can then decrypt the message with his or her private key and verify the signature with the sender's public key. Figure 4.11 shows this two-step process.

Figure 4.11 Example of Signing and Encrypting an E-Mail

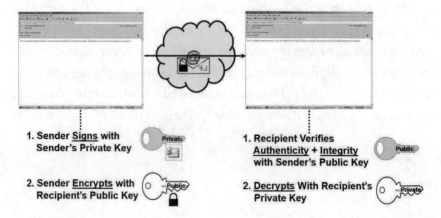

Encrypting and signing messages in this fashion requires senders and recipients to obtain and verify each other's public keys. This is typically done by using digital certificates. A **digital certificate** (also known as a public key certificate or digital ID) is an electronic document used to prove ownership of a public key. The certificate includes information about the key, information about its owner's identity, and the digital signature of an entity that has verified that the certificate's contents are correct. A digital certificate can be obtained from (and verified by) a certificate authority or a web of trust (in which users verify each other). A public key can also be obtained from a trusted key server. A commonly used certificate authority is Symantec (which acquired Verisign) (http://www.symantec.com/digital-id).

While in some respects a cumbersome process, signing and encrypting is not difficult after public keys have been exchanged. For example, in Microsoft Outlook, signing and encrypting an e-mail only involves checking two boxes and the message is automatically decrypted and authenticated at the user's end. See Electronic Communications, Chapter 9. The most challenging part is obtaining key pairs, exchanging public keys, and setting them up in the e-mail program for encryption.

There are now various services that provide easy-to-use options for secure e-mail and secure document exchange. They are discussed in Chapters 9 and 10.

BACKUP AND KEY RECOVERY

Because encryption on servers, desktops, laptops, tablets, smartphones, portable devices, etc. is an additional function that can sometimes fail, it is important to maintain a backup in a secure location of the data on encrypted devices. This is a best practice even when these kinds of devices are not encrypted.

It is also important to keep a copy of the key and store it in a safe place off the device. The backed-up key can be used for decryption if a password or passphrase is forgotten. It will also sometimes work if there is a failure of hardware or software. A symmetric key looks like this:

Figure 4.12 Sample Symmetric Key

+30NbBBMy7+1BumpfmN8QPHrwQr36/vBvaFLgQM561Q=

It can be saved on media like a desktop, laptop, or portable media (hopefully secure). In some instances, it can even be saved on paper.

In an enterprise setting like a law firm, it is best to actively manage encryption centrally on firm servers. Using tools like Microsoft Active Directory or enterprise encryption management products, backups of keys, along with alternate recovery keys, can be available to IT staff or service providers. While a complete discussion of enterprise solutions for enterprise management of encryption is beyond the scope of this book, some examples are discussed in Chapters 5 and 6.

CONCLUSION

This is a brief overview of the basics of encryption. While it is helpful for attorneys to understand these basics, an understanding is not necessary in order to use encryption. If you didn't take the time and effort to understand this chapter, it's ok. You don't need to understand encryption to use it. Once you get qualified help in setting up encryption, you'll be able to use it. Many of today's solutions make it easy to use—and many of the solutions won't strain your bank account.

> ## There's also an App for Android Users
> It's called Easy Decoder Ring and is free in Google Play (includes ads). It uses AES encryption and lets users encrypt and decrypt data entered in it. Here's a screenshot of it, using a user-selected passphrase.

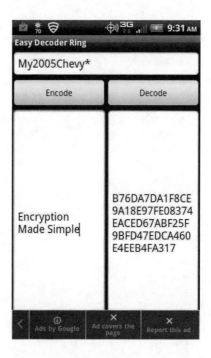

Chapter 5

ENCRYPTING LAPTOPS, DESKTOPS, AND SERVERS

Encryption can protect data on laptops, desktops and servers. It is most important for laptops because of their portability and risk of loss or theft. It takes some effort and ability with technology to set up encryption, but it's then pretty easy to use it. Particularly important during setup is backing up in a secure location the recovery key and backing up the data on the hard drive.

Many of today's encryption options, discussed in this chapter and the rest of the book, are inexpensive and easy to use, particularly after they have been installed. In the past, encryption was sometimes expensive and difficult to use, and had a noticeable effect on performance, particularly on older computers. Many options for desktops and laptops have no noticeable effect on performance. Encryption for servers and enterprise management is more expensive and requires more effort, but is being increasingly adopted.

Encryption is tied to an authorized user's logon credentials (username, plus password, passphrase, or other authentication, like a fingerprint). When the user logs on with the correct credentials, the program automatically accesses **the key** to decrypt the data. When he or she log offs or shuts down, the data is automatically encrypted.

Encryption Keys

Encryption keys are discussed in more detail in Chapter 4. For those who skipped Chapter 4, here's a summary.

Encryption keys are used to implement encryption for a specific user or users. A key is just a line or set of data that is used with an encryption program to encrypt and decrypt the data. Protection is provided by use of a mathematical formula in the encryption program (called an algorithm) with the unique key or keys.

The process is called **secret key** or **symmetric key encryption** where the same key is used to both encrypt and decrypt the data. With secret key encryption, it is critical to protect the security of the key because it can be used by anyone with access to it to decrypt the data. Secret key encryption is generally used to protect desktops, laptops, and portable media.

For a simplified comparison to the physical world, encryption is like a lock, the algorithm is like the internal mechanism of the lock, and the encryption key is like a physical key that locks and unlocks it.

Encryption of a desktop, laptop, or portable device is actually easier to use than a physical lock. The key is automatically accessed to decrypt the data when a user enters his or her log-on credentials. When the user logs off or the computer times out or is shut down, the data is automatically encrypted.

Because most encryption programs are tied to a user's password, **secure passwords or passphrases** are essential, and a forgotten password can lead to lost data.

Secure Passwords and Passphrases

Current recommendations for strong passwords or passphrases include the following:

- Minimum length of 14 characters.*
- Contain lower and upper case letters
- Include numbers

- Include a symbol or symbols

- Avoid dictionary words

* For years, the recommended length of passwords and passphrases was eight characters. Recent research has shown that they can be easily defeated with the use of today's computing power, including use of video cards. This has led to recommendations of minimums of 12 characters and, later, 14 characters. Requirement of a 14-character minimum is not yet common in businesses and law firms, but many are moving toward it.

A passphrase uses words that are easier to remember than a random password. Here's an example:

iluvmy2005BMW!

This one meets all of the recommendations.

Automatic logoff, after a specified time, is critical so that unencrypted data will not be exposed if a user goes away from a computer or forgets to turn it off. As an alternative, you can also configure the computer to automatically lock after a period of inactivity. This is normally done by configuring a screen saver lock. In an enterprise environment, like a law firm, access by an administrator, ability to reset passwords, backup, and key recovery are essential. Installing encryption and administering it, particularly in a large enterprise, can be a challenge.

DISK ENCRYPTION BASICS

There are two basic approaches to encrypting data on hard drives: full disk encryption and limited encryption. As its name suggests, full disk encryption protects the entire hard drive. It automatically encrypts everything and provides decrypted access when an authorized user properly logs in. Limited encryption protects only specified files or folders or a part of the drive. With limited encryption, the user has to elect to encrypt the specific data by saving it in an encrypted partition or folder. Because it can be easy to forget to put confidential data in an encrypted partition or file, full disk encryption is usually more secure and therefore recommended.

There are three options for protecting laptops and portable devices with encryption: hardware encryption, operating system encryption (such as Windows and Apple OS X), and encryption software.

All hard drive manufacturers now offer drives with hardware full disk encryption, called Self-Encrypting Drives (SED). There are encrypted options available for both traditional hard drives and newer solid state drives. The major laptop manufacturers all offer models with hardware encryption. Hardware encryption is generally easier to use and administer than encryption software. Some examples of drives with hardware encryption are Seagate Secure and Momentus (www.seagate.com), Hitachi Self-Encrypting Drives (www.hgst.com), Western Digital (www.wdc.com), CMS Products (www.cesecure.com), SanDisk (solid state) (www.sandisk.com), and Imation (www.imation.com). Secure use simply requires enabling encryption and setting a strong password or passphrase. The contents of the drive are automatically decrypted when an authorized user logs in. It is automatically encrypted when the user logs off or the laptop is turned off.

A recent article[1] described self-encrypting drives a security "best-kept secret," noting:

> SEDs are one of the information security industry's best kept secrets. They solve many common data loss problems, are easy to use and manage with minimal impact on system performance. Yet relatively few businesses and governments use SEDs, according to Robert Thibadeau, who assembled the original team at disk-maker Seagate, the company that pioneered SED technology.

---

1   Warwick Ashford, "Self-Encrypting Drives: SED the Best-Kept Secret in Hard Drive Encryption Security," *ComputerWeekly* (www.computerweekly.com/feature/Self-encrypting-drives-SED-the-best-kept-secret-in-hard-drive-encryption-security), last visited October 15, 2014.

At the most basic level, SEDs provide hardware-based data security by continuously scrambling data using a key, as it is written to the drive, and then descrambling the data with the key as the data is retrieved, giving users a high level of data protection.

The contents of an SED is always encrypted and the encryption keys are themselves encrypted and protected in hardware that cannot be accessed by other parts of the system. Because disk encryption is handled in the drive, overall system performance is not affected and is not subject to attacks targeting other components of the system.

Some IT professionals have recommended avoiding SED encryption because of concerns that data may be more difficult or impossible to recover in the event of a drive failure. They recommend encryption using one of the other options. With SEDs, backup of the data is particularly important.

Dell and Hewlett-Packard (HP) offer security suites that provide encryption, strong authentication, and additional security features. Dell's security package is called Dell Data Protection. It includes a number of separate options, ranging from strong authentication and encryption for a single desktop or laptop, to enterprise and cloud-management tools (http://www.dell.com/learn/us/en/19/campaigns/dell-data-protection-solutions). HP's suite is called ProtectTools. It also offers a number of options, from protection of an individual desktop or laptop, to central enterprise management (http://h20331.www2.hp.com/hpsub/cache/281822-0-0-225-121.html).

ENCRYPTION IN OPERATING SYSTEMS

Current business versions of Windows and current versions of Apple OS X have built-in encryption capability.

Windows

Windows Vista Enterprise and Ultimate and Windows 7 Enterprise and Ultimate, and Windows 8 and 8.1 Professional and

Enterprise include an encryption feature called BitLocker. Bit-Locker works below the Windows operating system and encrypts an entire volume on the hard drive. This means that when the drive is encrypted, the encryption protects the operating system as well as all software and data on the drive. For versions of Windows that do not support BitLocker, software encryption, discussed below, can be used.

On versions before Windows 8.1, BitLocker required either a computer that is equipped with a Trusted Platform Module (TPM) chip or use of an external USB drive to hold the decryption key. A TPM module is a security chip on the computer's motherboard that supports encryption. If a user plans to use BitLocker on a computer, it is important to select one that has a TPM chip that meets the current specification. Check the hardware requirements for the version of Windows that you are using and compare it with the specifications for the desktop or laptop. Or ask someone for advice—the major PC manufacturers have chat features on their websites to answer questions about their products. Use of a key on a USB drive is less secure because encryption can be defeated if an intruder gains access to the USB key. With Windows 8.1, there's another alternative for BitLocker with computers that don't have a TPM chip. It can be set up directly on the computer, but it requires a pre-boot passphrase that accesses the decryption key. This means that a user has to enter a pre-boot passphrase, then log into Windows. A user can set up the same passphrase for both, but it has to be entered twice, once for pre-boot and once for logging in.

The business versions of Windows also include an encryption function called Encrypting File System (EFS). It allows encryption of files and folders. An authorized user who is logged in has access to decrypted data. It is encrypted and unreadable to anyone else (unless they can defeat the login process). EFS is considered a fairly weak encryption method that is easily cracked using forensic tools. You are better off using BitLocker or one of the other third-party encryption products discussed below.

Setup of BitLocker is fairly technical. For many attorneys, it will be necessary to obtain technical assistance to implement it. There are instructions on Microsoft's website. During setup, there is a set of dialog boxes that take a user through the process. The instructions are available at:

- Windows 8.1: http://windows.microsoft.com/en-us/windows-8/bitlocker-drive-encryption.
- Windows 7: http://windows.microsoft.com/en-us/windows/protect-files-bitlocker-drive-encryption#1TC=windows-7.
- Vista: http://windows.microsoft.com/en-us/windows/protect-files-bitlocker-drive-encryption#1TC=windows-vista.

The BitLocker setup instructions include the following warning:

> **Warning:** When you turn on BitLocker for the first time, make sure you create a recovery key. Otherwise, you could permanently lose access to your files.

A Bitlocker recovery key is a line or set of data that can be backed up to a Microsoft account, a law firm network, or another computer. It can also be printed on paper. Make sure that the backup location is secure or the recovery key could be used to compromise the encryption. A BitLocker recovery key looks like this:

609430-136796-639472-379917-216106-640223-465533-702097

When backing up the recovery key, the drive identifier will be saved in the text file along with the actual BitLocker recovery key. If you have multiple partitions on the hard disk or multiple drives, you need to back up the key for each partition and drive. When utilizing the recovery key, you will need to match the appropriate identifier code to the correct drive.

Windows 8.1 has an additional encryption option called Device Encryption. It's included in all versions of Windows 8.1, not just the business ones. It has very specific hardware requirements that most current PCs do not meet. It also requires InstantGo, a feature that allows a PC to instantly wake up. For information about these requirements and whether a PC meets them, compare the requirements on Microsoft's website with the manufacturer's specifications for the PC. Or ask someone for help.

Device Encryption is automatically enabled when a user with an administrator account logs on to a Microsoft account. The recovery key is automatically backed up to the Microsoft account. While this option provides strong security for a PC, there is a risk that an unauthorized person can defeat it by getting access to a user's Microsoft account and the recovery key.

Device Encryption can also be turned on manually and the recovery key backed up to a network with Active Directory (an administration tool for Windows networks). There does not currently appear to be an option for enabling Device Encryption without a Microsoft account or network with Active Directory (http://windows.microsoft.com/ en-us/windows-8/using-device-encryption).

Apple OS X

Older versions of Apple OS X have built-in file encryption in File-Vault. Newer versions, starting with Lion, have full disk encryption available in FileVault 2. Follow Apple's instructions for turning it on. After a password is set, it just requires turning on the FileVault button in System Preferences. Instructions are available at http:// support.apple.com/kb/ht4790. FileVault 2 also generates a recovery key that it prompts the user to store. It provides an option for storing it with Apple.

Recent advances have attacked Apple's encryption scheme, and the Passware software suite claims to be able to defeat FileVault 2 in less than an hour.[2] Even with the availability of forensic tools, a

---

2 However, in order to use this tool, you must have a physical memory image file (acquired while the encrypted volume was mounted). Unless you're a forensic technologist, you won't even know how to create the physical memory image file, which is a forensic image of the memory contents of a running computer.

laptop encrypted with FileVault is still far more secure than one without encryption.

ENCRYPTION SOFTWARE

The third option for disk encryption (in addition to self-encrypting drives and operating system encryption) is encryption software. Some commonly used third-party encryption software products for hard drives include those offered by Symantec (PGP and Endpoint; www.symantec.com), McAfee (Endpoint Encryption; www.mcafee. com), Check Point (ZoneAlarm DataLock; (www.zonealarm.com), WinMagic (SecureDoc; www.winmagic.com), and Sophos (Safe-Guard; www.sophos.com). These vendors all have options available for Macs.

The following is a screen shot of the log-on screen of a computer protected with WinMagic's SecureDoc:

Figure 5.1 SecureDoc Log-on Screen

Most encryption solutions have single sign-on options, where entry of the logon credentials automatically enters the user for Windows or OS X.

An open-source encryption program that was formerly widely used is TrueCrypt (www.truecrypt.org). However, it has been discontinued and should no longer be relied upon. Its developers have posted the following on the TrueCrypt website: "WARNING: Using TrueCrypt is not secure as it may contain unfixed security issues."

LAPTOPS

Of the computers covered in this chapter, laptops present the greatest threat of loss, theft, and unauthorized access, because they are compact and portable. They can easily be lost or stolen outside the office. They also present the greatest risk inside an office because they are small, portable, and expensive, so they present an attractive target if physical security fails. This section covers laptops. Encryption of smartphones and tablets is included in the next chapter.

Many laptop vendors offer biometric access (fingerprint reader) to facilitate encryption of the hard disk. This avoids the use of passwords or passphrases at boot up. The fingerprint is used in lieu of a password. You should configure as least two fingerprints (one on each hand) in addition to a backup boot password or passphrase should the fingerprint reader fail. A best practice would be to register two fingers from each hand (four total fingerprints).

The major laptop vendors all offer models with self-encrypting drives and with the business versions of Windows that include Bit-Locker and with TPM chips. Apple's current OS X on Mac laptops includes FileVault 2. The easiest way to protect laptops is generally with hardware level encryption or BitLocker or FileVault. The third-party encryption software products, discussed earlier in this chapter, are also options for encrypting laptops.

Except for solos and small firms, enterprise management of encrypted devices, including laptops, is highly recommended.

DESKTOPS

Some law firms that are at the leading edge of security are encrypting desktops, going beyond encryption of laptops. In addition, some clients in regulated industries, like financial services, are requesting or requiring attorneys to encrypt their data on desktops as well as on laptops and portable media. While not yet a standard practice, it provides for strong security. There is a much greater risk of loss or theft with devices that are regularly used outside of offices, but there have been incidents of burglaries and insider thefts that have involved desktop computers. The risk of stolen desktops has increased as they have become more compact, including all-in-one models.

Desktops can be encrypted with all three options discussed above: self-encrypting drives, operating system encryption, or encryption software.

SERVERS

Encryption is a security measure that is increasingly being employed to protect confidential data on servers. They often process and store very high volumes of sensitive data. As with desktops, some clients are also requesting or requiring attorneys to encrypt their data stored on servers. While a discussion of server security is beyond the scope of this book, it is a safeguard that attorneys should explore with their IT staff and consultants.

ENTERPRISE MANAGEMENT

As we noted in Chapter 4, it is best in an enterprise setting such as a law firm to actively manage encryption centrally on firm servers.

Using tools like Microsoft Active Directory or enterprise encryption management products, password resetting (if a password is forgotten), backups of keys, along with alternate recovery keys, can be available to IT staff or service providers. Symantec, McAfee, Checkpoint, WinMagic, and Sophos (discussed above) as well as Dell (Dell Data Protection | Encryption Enterprise Edition, www. dell.com/us/business/p/ddpe-enterprise-edition/pd), offer enterprise management solutions.

WinMagic, a leading supplier of encryption software products, offers SecureDoc Enterprise Server (SES), which combines security-related management on a centralized enterprise server. It can manage policies, password rules, and encryption, including SecureDoc's software encryption for PCs, Windows (BitLocker), Apple's OS X (FileVault 2), and encryption with Self Encrypting Drives. This screenshot shows the management console that administrators can use to centrally manage all encrypted devices, including accessing recovery keys.

Figure 5.2 SecureDoc Enterprise Management Console

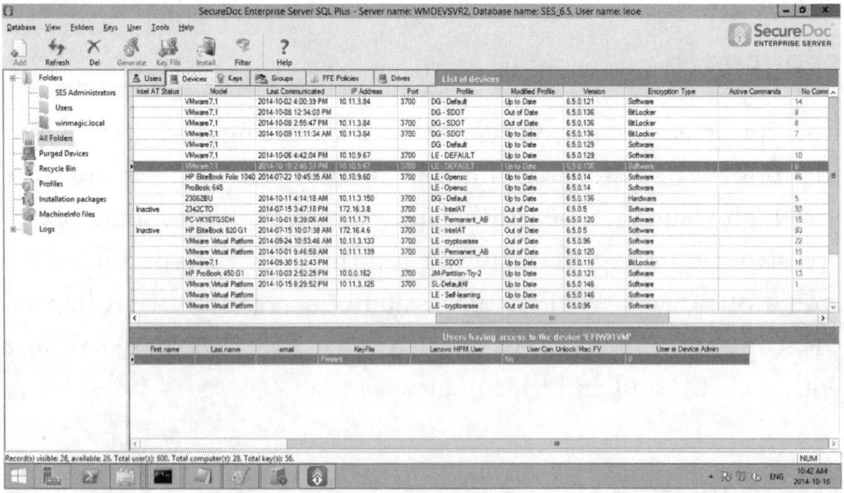

CONCLUSION

Encryption provides strong protection for data on laptops, desktops, and servers. It is most important for laptops because of their portability and risk of loss or theft. For laptops, encryption has been described as a security "no brainer" and attorneys should be using it. Encryption of desktops and servers is increasing, but is not yet a standard practice for attorneys and law firms. It takes some effort and ability with technology to set encryption up (and many attorneys will need help), but it's then pretty easy to use encryption.

"Military Grade Encryption"

The phrase "military grade encryption," and similar terms are sometimes used in advertising for encryption programs and encrypted products. They're generally just marketing terms and don't have a uniform meaning. They may just mean that the encryption is based on an encryption formula (algorithm) that has been approved for military encryption. They do not necessarily mean that the encryption has been properly implemented or tested.

A more meaningful phrase is compliance with the Federal Information Processing Standard (FIPS). FIPS is a set of technical standards for U.S. government agencies (non-military). A number of FIPS standards cover encryption. A common one is FIPS 140-2, Security Requirements for Cryptographic Modules. Encryption validated under this standard has been tested to establish that the product or application (or the encryption module used in it) is in compliance with this standard. The standard covers four levels of security, with Level 1 being the lowest and Level 4 the highest.

There is no set FIPS 140-2 level for attorneys and law firms, but the higher the level, the greater security it provides. FIPS compliance is generally not a requirement for law firms unless they are working with government contractors, but they may be used as guides.

Chapter 6

ENCRYPTION FOR SMARTPHONES AND TABLETS

The attributes that make smartphones and tablets great productivity tools also make them risky. They are mobile, compact, powerful, have large storage capacity, and have multiple avenues of connectivity. But they can be lost or stolen, hacked, infected by malware, and have their communications intercepted—all exposing confidential data. As discussed previously, encryption is a "no-brainer" solution that provides strong protection in the event of loss or theft. On today's smartphones and tablets, encryption is generally easy to set up and use.

Loss or theft is a great threat. *Consumer Reports* has estimated that approximately 3.1 million Americans were victims of smartphone theft during 2012 and that about 1.4 million smartphones were lost and not recovered.[1] The Federal Communications Commission reported in April 2012 that 30 to 40 percent of robberies in major cities in the U.S. involved cell phones.[2] The *New York Times*

---

1 www.consumerreports.org/cro/news/2014/04/smart-phone-thefts-rose-to-3-1-million-last-year/index.htm (last updated May 28, 2014).

2 FCC Announcement (April 10, 2012) www.fcc.gov/document/announcement-new-initiatives-combat-smartphone-and-data-theft.

reported that over half of the robberies in San Francisco in 2012 involved a smartphone. It reported one instance when armed robbers asked a woman for her iPhone, then handed it back when they saw that it wasn't the latest model.[3]

Symantec, a leading security company, conducted a limited study in which it placed 50 "lost" smartphones in public places and tracked what happened to them.[4] It reported that, "When a business-connected mobile device is lost, there is more than an 80 percent chance that an attempt will be made to breach corporate data and/or networks" and only 50 percent of the finders contacted the owner and provided contact information.

SECURE SETUP

Encryption is part of the basic security setup that is generally recommended by security professionals, device manufacturers, and government agencies for smartphones and tablets.[5] These basic measures include:

- Review and follow the security instructions of the device manufacturer and carrier. (An important step that is often forgotten or ignored. Most Quick Start Guides do not adequately address security. See below for references to some of these security guides.)
- Maintain physical control of the device.
- Set a strong password, passphrase, or PIN.
- Set locking after a set number of failed log-on attempts.
- Set automatic logoff after a defined time.
- Encrypt confidential data on the device and any storage card. (May require third-party software on older devices.)

---

3   Malia Wollan, "Outsmarting Smartphone Thieves," *New York Times* (May 8, 2013).

4   "The Symantec Smartphone Honey Stick Project" (2012).

5   See Roberto Baldwin, "Don't Be Silly. Lock Down and Encrypt Your Smartphone," *Wired* (October 26, 2014).

- Provide for protection of data in transit, including secure wired and wireless connections.
- Disable interfaces that are not being used. (Bluetooth, Wi-Fi, etc.)
- Enable remote location, locking, and wiping of a lost device.
- Consider use of third-party security applications. (antivirus, encryption, remote locating, and wiping, etc.)
- Backup important data.
- Do not "jailbreak" or "root" a smartphone. (These actions unlock a phone, including security controls.)

Current iPhones, iPads, Android phones and tablets, BlackBerry devices, and some Windows mobile phones all have built-in encryption that is easy to use. It's either automatic (with a password or PIN) or simply requires turning encryption on.

Apple has included device encryption since the iPhone 3GS. It's turned on automatically when a PIN or password is set. Apple recently announced that, starting with the current iOS 8, it will no longer have access to encryption keys—they will be stored only on the devices. Apple has stated that this change will prevent it from decrypting devices for law enforcement and government agencies. If it works that way, it will provide strong protection unless the PIN or password can be bypassed. It will not protect backed-up data off the device (e.g., data synced to the iCloud).

Google Android devices have provided on-device encryption for a number of years. It has been available with Honeycomb (tablets), Ice Cream Sandwich, and later versions of the operating system. Some later implementations of Gingerbread also support on-device encryption. Earlier versions require a third-party app for encryption. Google has recently announced that it will no longer have access to encryption keys. Like iOS, they will be stored only on the phone. On current Androids, encryption has to be turned on for both the device and storage cards, a simple setting. With Android

Lollipop, which was released in late 2014, encryption is automatically enabled when a PIN, password, or pattern is set.

Windows Phone 7 does not support on-device encryption. Windows Phone 8 does support on-device encryption, but it cannot be turned on by an individual user. Encryption can only be turned on with Exchange Active Sync or a mobile device management/enterprise mobility management program on a network. Windows RT and Windows 8.1 on tablets have encryption enabled by default for devices that meet published Microsoft technical specifications.

BlackBerry has been considered the "gold standard" for security for years, including encryption. It takes a simple setting to enable it. It can be enabled on the device itself or remotely via a BlackBerry Enterprise Server.

The steps for basic secure setup of the common mobile operating systems include the following.

iPhones

For iPhones, follow the instructions in "Security Features" in Chapter 3: Basics in the *iPhone User Guide* (iOS 8) (September, 2014).[6] They include:

- In "Settings" > "Touch ID & Passcode" or "Passcode," turn off "Simple Passcode." (A Simple Passcode enables encryption, but is not recommended because it is too easy to defeat.)
- Set "Passcode Lock" and choose a strong passcode (enables encryption).
- Set "Auto-Lock."
- Set "Erase Data" (after ten failed passcode attempts, securely removes data).
- Turn on "Find My Phone" (in Mobile Setting or iCloud).

---

6   Current version *available at* http://support.apple.com/manuals. See also Apple, *iOS Security* (February 2014).

- In iTunes (on the desktop or laptop), turn on "Encrypt iPhone backup."

In addition,

- Set Siri to off when the phone is passcode locked.[7]

Encryption is automatically enabled when a PIN or password is set.

iPads

For iPads, follow the instructions in "Security" in Chapter 3: Basics in the *iPad User Guide* (iOS 8) (September, 2014).[8] Recommended security settings include:

- In Settings, General, Passcode Lock:
  - Turn off "Simple Passcode" (allows a complex Passcode longer than four numbers).
  - Select "Turn Passcode On" and set a strong passcode (requires Passcode to access iPad and enables Data Protection encryption).
  - Set "Require Passcode" to "immediately" or a short time.
  - Turn on "Erase Data" (erases data after ten failed attempts to enter Passcode).
- In "Settings, General, Auto-Lock," set a short idle time (after which re-entry of Passcode is required.)
- In "Settings, iCloud," turn on "Find My iPad" (allows use of iPhone app or Internet to display the iPad's location on a map, to display a screen message on the iPad, and to remotely lock or wipe the iPad).
- In "Settings, General, Bluetooth," turn "Bluetooth" off when you're not using it.
- In "Settings, WI-Fi," turn "Wi-Fi" off when you're not using it.

---

7   www.pcworld.com/article/242253/siris_security_hole_the_passcode_is_the_problem.html.

8   Current version *available at* http://support.apple.com/manuals.

- When using a wireless network, check for a "lock icon"—indicating a secured wireless network. Avoid unsecure wireless networks or take appropriate precautions to protect your iPad and confidential data. Using a cellular network is much more secure than using an unsecured wireless network.
- For Internet browsing, in "Settings, Safari," turn on "Fraud Warning" and "Block Pop-Ups."
- To protect data backed up in *iTunes*, connect to *iTunes*, in the "iTunes Summary" screen, select "Encrypt iPad backup."

Encryption is automatically enabled when a PIN or password is set.

Android

For Android smartphones and tablets, follow the security set up instructions in the device manufacturer's manual.[9] They should include:

- Set Screen Lock (password or PIN) (in Settings > Security).
- Set Screen Timeout (in Settings > Security).
- Enable remote locating and remote lock and erase in Android Device Manager (in Apps > Google Settings).
- Encrypt Phone or Tablet (in Settings > Security). Encryption can take an hour or more when it is enabled for the first time. **Caution:** Connect the phone or tablet to a charger during the encryption process when encryption is enabled for the first time. Loss of power during the encryption process may result in a loss of data. Backup before encrypting. **Another caution:** On some devices, turning on encryption for the SD card after the device has been in use will wipe the data on the card. If this is the case, there will be a warning when encryption is being set up. Pay attention during the

---

9   E.g., Google's encryption instructions for the Nexus phone, https://support.google.com/nexus/answer/2844831?hl=en.

encryption setup process. Users will usually not want to encrypt the card if the data on it will be erased.

The layout and specific steps can vary with different Android versions and device manufacturers. This is an example, just making two checks to enable encryption—one for the device and one for the memory card.

Figure 6.1 Enabling Encryption on Current Androids Requires Checking Two Boxes

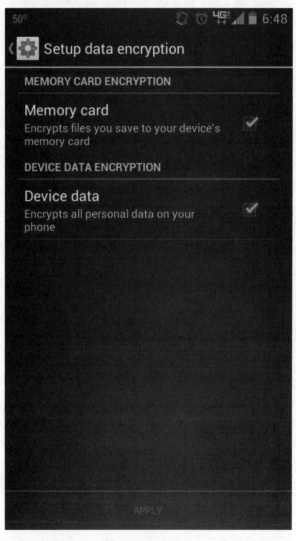

BlackBerry

The current version of the BlackBerry operating system is Blackberry 10 OS. BlackBerry's robust security features have to be turned on to provide the available protection. Most law firms and other enterprises that use BlackBerry's manage security settings through BlackBerry Enterprise Server. Like other smartphones, the following security settings should be enabled, in Settings > Security and Privacy: set a strong PIN or password, set locking after a period of inactivity, turn on encryption (device and media card), and set up BlackBerry Protect (for remote locating and wiping).[10]

Windows

Windows RT is a version of Windows that was designed for tablets and ultra-notebooks. It has been used for the Microsoft Surface tablet and for devices by others like Dell and Asus. It has had limited commercial success. Windows RT includes encryption called Device Encryption that is automatically enabled when a user with an administrator account logs on to a Microsoft account. The Surface Pro 3 uses Windows 8.1. Device Protection is enabled by default on Windows 8.1 devices that have a defined set of hardware specifications, including Surface Pro 3s.

With both Windows RT and 8.1, the user is prompted to save a recovery key during the set-up process. The recovery key may be saved in the user's Microsoft account on a network (like a law firm's) that is set up to manage Windows mobile devices, on a portable device, like a USB drive, or printed on paper. This is an important step because the recovery key will be needed for access if the password is forgotten and may be needed if there is an operating system failure. Some users have reported that they have had to use their recovery keys during upgrades. Consult and follow Microsoft's instructions for setting up security, including Device Encryption.

---

10 Instructions at: http://docs.blackberry.com/en/smartphone_users/deliverables/47561/als 1334342592773.jsp.

MOBILE DEVICE MANAGEMENT

In an enterprise environment like a law firm, some form of mobile device management (MDM) is frequently used in addition to the security measures applied to each device. MDM is a set of controls that provides for enterprise control (by IT staff or a service provider) of secure setup and use of mobile devices. MDM can implement settings or force users to employ security requirements, like complexity and age of passwords and encryption. MDM can also be used to locate and wipe lost or stolen devices. The tools can be used for storing encryption recovery keys and providing alternative administrator access to encrypted mobile devices. MDM has been evolving into Enterprise Mobility Management (EMM), which adds features like data protection and application control. A number of service providers have products and services in this area, either as a tool for the enterprise to install and operate or as hosted services.

Examples of leading MDM service providers include AirWatch (VMware) (www.air-watch.com), Citrix (Xenmobile) (www.citrix.com), Good Technology (www.good.com), IBM (MaaS360) (www.maas360.com), and MobilIron (www.mobileiron.com).

While it is not a full-featured MDM solution, Microsoft Exchange ActiveSync can be used to synchronize Outlook data with mobile devices over a secure channel and to enforce some security controls, including device encryption (www.microsoft.com/exchange/en-us/default.aspx). It can be used to synch Outlook e-mail, contacts, calendar, and tasks and to require the use of passwords and encryption. It includes some management capability, but lacks some MDM functions. For example, its management capability varies by device, its management tools are fragmented, it lacks built-in reporting, and it does not have mobile app management capability. Its functionality and support for it in mobile platforms have been growing over time. Many solo and small firm attorneys use the limited capabilities of Exchange ActiveSync instead of investing in the more expensive MDM solutions.

ENCRYPTED COMPARTMENT FOR LAW FIRM DATA

A "compartment," or "sandbox," on a smartphone or tablet is a configuration of the device that puts enterprise (law firm) apps and data in a separate partition of the device from personal apps or data. The compartment is encrypted and isolated from the rest of the device to protect the enterprise apps and data.

Good Technology, a leading MDM service provider, offers strong management and security for mobile devices. It includes a secure compartment that separates enterprise applications and data from personal ones, encrypts it, and requires a password for access to the enterprise compartment. It can remotely wipe the contents of the compartment or all data on the device. It has been certified for certain uses under the security requirements of the Federal Information Processing Standard (FIPS) for federal agencies. Other MDM providers have been adding this capability.

BlackBerry 10 and Samsung Knox have the built-in capability to separate business and personal apps and data. Business apps and data are contained in a secure partition that is isolated from the rest of the phone, similar to Good Technology's add-on. Samsung devices require a compatible MDM to enable the secure compartment. Android Lollipop, released late in 2014, includes a feature to separate business and personal data.

CONCLUSION—USING THE "NO-BRAINER" SOLUTION

Because of the risk and high incidence of loss and theft, smartphones and tablets present a great danger of compromise of confidential information stored on them. Fortunately, there's "a no-brainer" solution—encryption. It's built into most modern devices. It just has to be turned on.

Chapter 7
ENCRYPTING PORTABLE DRIVES

As with smartphones and tablets, the attributes that make USB flash drives (thumb drives) and external hard drives so useful also make them very dangerous. They are compact and have large storage capacity and have been increasing in capacity while they have become more compact and decreased in price. But they can be easily lost or stolen, exposing large volumes of confidential data.

USB flash drives now come in capacities as large as three TB and capacities just keep growing. External hard drives now equal capacities of internal hard drives in computers, as high as four TB, and also keep growing. They can store huge volumes of data that needs to be protected.

As previously noted, encryption is viewed as a "no-brainer" security measure that provides strong protection in the event of loss or theft of portable devices. Encryption solutions are readily available, inexpensive, and generally easy to set up and use. Encryption can make the difference between a simple loss of hardware and a data breach exposing confidential data. This is evident from these examples: (1) the laptop and external drive stolen from a the car of an employee of the

Department of Veterans Affairs,[1] (2) the law firm hard drive left on the Baltimore light rail,[2] and (3) the drive recently stolen from the car of the employee of a Georgia law firm[3]—resulting in data breaches from unencrypted devices. In these and many other incidents, the data would have been protected if it had been encrypted.

Like hard drives in computers, portable drives, both USB flash drives and external hard drives, can be protected by built-in hardware encryption or software encryption. Software encryption can be pre-installed on the drive or added by Windows (BitLocker to Go), Apple's OS X (FileVault 2), or by third-party encryption products.

ENCRYPTED USB FLASH DRIVES

Individual USB drives are available with built-in encryption. Examples include the CMS Secure Vault (www.cesecure.com), IronKey (www.imation.com), Kanguru Defender and Micro (www.kanguru. com), Kingston Data Traveler (www.kingston.com), and SanDisk Cruzer Professional and Cruzer Enterprise (www.sandisk.com). Available products keep changing. They are readily available from office supply stores and online. Check the reviews for others' experience with the current options.

Thumb drives with encryption look no different from unencrypted ones. The difference is "under the hood":

Figure 7.1 CMS Products CE Vault Flash Drive

---

1   "Laptop stolen from VA contractor contains veterans' personal data." NextGov. http://www.next gov.com/health/2010/05/laptop-stolen-from-va-contractor-contains-veterans-personal-data/ 46684/. Accessed October 19, 2014.

2   "Law firm loses hard drive with patient records." *Baltimore Sun.* http://articles.baltimoresun. com/2011-10-10/news/bs-md-stent-hard-drive-20111010_1_patient-records-law-firm-medical- records. Accessed October 19, 2014.

3   "Backup hard drive stolen from law firm contained personal info." *SC Magazine.* http://www.sc magazine.com/backup-hard-drive-stolen-from-law-firm-contained-personal-info/article/368427/. Accessed October 19, 2014.

To enable encryption, follow the manufacturer's instructions and remember to back up the encryption key by saving it in a safe location off the device. After that, it's just a matter of using a password or passphrase to open the device. Here's an example:

Figure 7.2 IronKey Unlock Screen

The drive is decrypted when the password or passphrase is entered. It is encrypted when it is removed from a computer, it is closed, or the computer is shut down.

A note of caution: Some drives that use encryption software, rather than hardware, are fully encrypted after encryption has been enabled. Others have an encrypted portion, with the rest of the drive unencrypted. When you connect the drive to a computer, it may show up as two drives—one encrypted and the other not encrypted. Make sure that you understand and follow the directions.

Here's an example. Figure 7.3 shows a screenshot of the files on a SanDisk Cruzer Blade flash drive. It uses SanDisk SecureAccess encryption that is included with the drive. Files and data that are saved in the vault are protected with AES-128 encryption. Files and data on the rest of the drive are not encrypted (http:// www.sandisk.com/products/usb/drives/cruzer-blade). The Cruzer Blade comes in sizes from four GB to 64 GB and works with Windows and Macs.

Figure 7.3 SanDisk Secure Access Vault on USB Thumb Drive

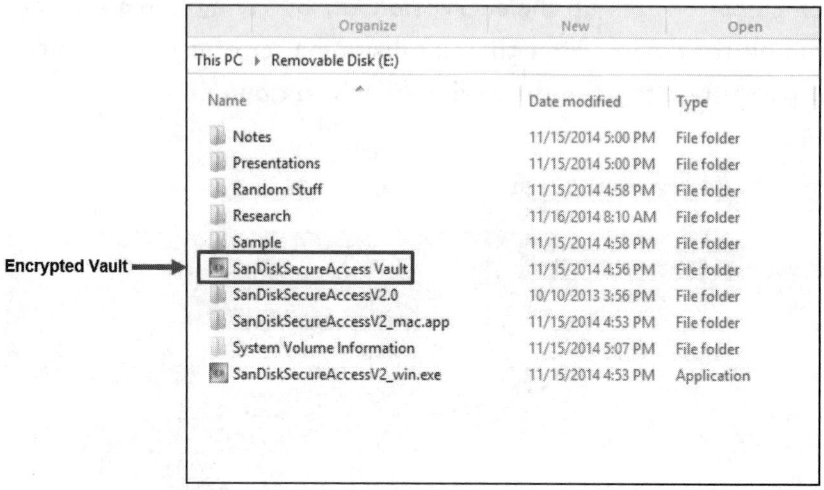

On any device that is not fully encrypted, it is critical to store confidential information in the encrypted part. Otherwise, it is not protected. Fully encrypted devices eliminate the risk of errors of storing confidential data outside the encrypted part.

The IronKey, by Imation, is a favorite of the authors. It includes strong encryption, wiping if the wrong credentials are entered too many times, and strong physical construction. As an added bonus, several of the models contain a secure password management application called Identity Manager. IronKey devices have a custom version of the Mozilla Firefox Internet browser installed on them. When it is connected to a computer and the Internet accessed through it, all of the browsing activity occurs on the IronKey instead of the computer. That is very secure browsing!

Figure 7.4 IronKey Encrypted USB Thumb Drive

Some models of the IronKey (the W300, W500, and W700) support Windows to Go (part of Windows 8.1 Enterprise) (www.micro soft.com/en-us/windows/enterprise/products-and-technologies/ devices/windowstogo.aspx). Windows to Go allows the IronKey to work as an image of a law firm or enterprise computer. When it is plugged into a supporting computer, like a home computer, all of the computing activity is securely done on the IronKey, basically using the computer like a terminal.

The Kingston Traveler Workspace (www.kingston.com/us/usb/ bootable#DTWS) and several drives by Spyrus (www.spyruswtg. com/wtg-features/#WorkSafe) also support Windows to Go. This is a new feature of Windows that has the potential for providing high security when away from the office—at home or on the road. It is new with Windows 8.1, so it is important to watch for reports about its utility and security.

The drive displayed in Figure 7.1 is a CMS Products CE Secure Vault Flash Drive. It has hardware encryption, using AES-256, which encrypts all data on the device. These drives range in capacity from eight GB to 32 GB and work on PCs and Macs. One of the authors has used CMS Products encrypted drives and secure backup products and has had good experience with them (http://www. cmsproducts.com/ce-secure-vault-hardware-encrypted-flash-drive).

A past experience with an early CMS Products encrypted USB drive provides an important lesson. It was purchased as a learning tool for the author's first foray into encrypted portable devices. After it was used for a while, then put aside for several months, the author forgot the password and couldn't locate where it had been written for backup. (Very secure, but not very productive.) CMS Products' Tech Support was able to restore the drive, so it could be used again, but all of the data on it was lost. This is the way that secure encryption should work. Fortunately, it was just test data. **It is critical to securely store the password and recovery key in a secure location off the device and to back up the data.**

ENCRYPTED EXTERNAL HARD DRIVES

External hard drives with built-in hardware encryption (self-encrypting drives) are similar to encrypted internal drives for laptops, as discussed in Chapter 5.

An example of an external hard drive with hardware encryption is the CMS Products CE-Secure DiskVault shown in Figure 7.5. It uses AES-256 encryption and is available in capacities from 120 GB to 960 GB. This model works only with Windows (www.cesecure.com).

Figure 7.5 CE-Secure DiskVault External Hard Drive

OPERATING SYSTEM ENCRYPTION OF PORTABLE DRIVES

Software encryption can be installed on compatible USB flash drives and external hard drives by using Windows BitLocker to Go or Apple's File Vault 2. BitLocker is available on Windows Vista and 7 (Ultimate and Enterprise) and Windows 8 and 8.1 (Professional and Enterprise).

ENCRYPTION SOFTWARE

Another option for encrypting portable devices is encryption software available from major security vendors. Some examples include McAfee Endpoint Encryption (www.mcafee.com), Sophos SafeGuard Easy (www.sophos.com), Symantec Endpoint Encryption and Whole Disk Encryption (www.symantec.com), and WinMagic Removable Media Encryption (www.winmagic.com).

Enterprise Management

As with laptops and desktops, it is best in an enterprise setting such as a law firm to actively manage encryption for portable drives centrally on firm servers. Some examples of options are discussed in Chapter 5.

CONCLUSION

Like laptops, USB drives and external hard drives present a high risk of data exposure through loss or theft. Encryption is a "no-brainer" security measure to protect against this risk. It's now widely available, inexpensive, and easy to use.

Chapter 8
NETWORK COMMUNICATIONS

It is important to protect data in transmission as it moves through the various networks from your device on the way to its final destination. Data travels over both wired and wireless networks in packets (distinct groupings of data) with source and destination information placed at the beginning of the data packet. Without encryption, it is relatively easy for an attacker to capture and reassemble packets with a program called a packet sniffer. There are several free packet sniffers available on the Internet with Wireshark being one of the most popular. On wired networks, the attacker has to be connected to the network (directly or remotely). On wireless networks, an attacker just has to be within range of the network. Protection can be provided by encrypting the data, providing an encrypted "tunnel" over a network or networks (also known as a Virtual Private Network, or VPN), or both.

With a network comprised of wire or fiber, you can provide some level of protection by securing how the media is routed including whether it is encased in piping, concrete, or some other physical protection. That only helps you for the routes that you install and control. Once it leaves your office network, it is much harder to provide physical protection.

In contrast, it is hard to protect something you can't see. At least with a fiber or wired network, you can visually inspect the network wiring to see if someone is trying to tap the line. Not so with wireless networks. The radio waves propagate to areas that are nearly impossible to monitor. So how do we protect these instances of data in transit? Yet again, encryption is your friend. If we encrypt the wireless data transmissions, the confidentiality of the data can be protected. There are various ways to encrypt wireless communications, from the very weak to the very strong.

A wireless device (e.g. computer, smartphone, tablet) can authenticate to an access point (think of this as a wireless receiver) in one of two ways. If open system authentication (OSA) is used, there is no requirement that the wireless device have a specific cryptographic key to present to the AP. In most cases, the wireless device only needs the correct SSID (wireless network name). There is no encryption here, so all the data is in clear text. By default, wireless devices operate using OSA.

The second way is through shared key authentication (SKA), where the access point (AP) sends a random value to the wireless device. The wireless device uses its cryptographic key to encrypt the value and returns it to the AP. The AP decrypts the information and compares it to the original value. If there is a match, you get connected.

There are three wireless network encryption standards known as WEP, WPA, and WPA2, which will be discussed below. If you are impatient and don't want to read the technical details of each, WPA2 is the only recommended standard.

WEP

Wireless Equivalent Privacy (WEP) is a very common way to encrypt wireless transmissions. WEP is a standard that adds security to 802.11 wireless networks. It was ratified in September of

1999. It operates at the data link (layer two) of the OSI (Open Systems Interconnection) model (there are seven total layers). Don't worry, there will not be a test concerning the OSI model. All you need to know is that, since WEP works at the lower layer of the model, it does not provide end-to-end security.

The key thing to know about WEP is that the security is extremely weak and that there are free tools available to crack the WEP encryption. This means that you should *not* use WEP as a protection method for wireless transmissions. If you are not interested in how WEP works or the specific "failures" of WEP, you can stop reading this section and jump over to the next encryption method.

There are three core deficiencies of the WEP protocol. The first is the use of static encryption keys. The WEP protocol uses the RC4 algorithm, which is a stream-symmetric cipher. Symmetric means that the exact same key is used by both the sender and receiver to encrypt and decrypt the data. The 802.11 standard does not specify how to automatically update the keys so in most cases the RC4 symmetric keys are never changed. To make matters worse, all of the wireless devices and access points usually have the same key. This is similar to everyone in your firm using the same password for network logon. Not a good thing.

The second problem with WEP deals with how initialization vectors (IV) are used. An initialization vector is a numeric value that is used as a seed value. This value is used with the symmetric key and the RC4 algorithm to make the encryption process more variable or random. Having an encryption scheme that is very random helps to keep the data secure since it would be very difficult to decipher any patterns. If you can determine the pattern, the bad guys may be able to understand the encryption process and actually determine the encryption key. The initialization value and symmetric key are applied to the RC4 algorithm in order to generate a key stream. Think of the key stream as the flow of data in an encrypted state.

Not to get too much in the weeds, but there is some binary magic that happens next, which results in ciphertext (encryption). In most of the WEP implementations, the same initialization value vector is used time and time again. In addition, since the same symmetric key is also typically used, there is no effective randomness in the data stream. Since the data stream is not random, thereby having patterns, there is the possibility to reverse-engineer the process to determine the encryption key. You can then decrypt the data when you are armed with the encryption key. In fact, many of the free tools that are available on the Internet do exactly that. AirSnort, aircrack-ng, and WEP-Crack are examples of these cracking tools.

The third issue with WEP has to do with the Integrity Check Value (ICV), which is essentially a 32-bit check value to see if the data was modified or damaged during the transmission. The sender and receiver calculate the ICV. The receiver compares the values and rejects the frame if the values are different. There are certain situations where an attacker can modify the data and the receiver will not detect that an alteration occurred. That essentially makes the method of verifying data integrity worthless.

Hopefully, you can now see why WEP encryption is not an option to protect wireless transmissions. But what should you do to protect a wireless network? Read on to learn about other wireless encryption methods.

WPA

In order to address the security flaws with WEP, the wireless standard was modified. One of the specified changes was known as Wi-Fi Protected Access or WPA. WPA is sometimes referred to as the draft 802.11i standard and was available in 2003. An important improvement is the use of Temporal Key Integrity Protocol (TKIP). With WEP, the encryption key is configured once and used for all communication packets. TKIP vastly improves this by creating a new dynamic key for each and every packet transmitted. Remember that effective encryption is dependent on the randomness of the ciphertext. You can't get much more random than changing the key for each packet.

WPA also included improvement in the integrity checking process. WPA uses the Michael message integrity code (MIC) instead of the ICV used with WEP encryption. Using a MIC ensures that the receiver can detect if the data from the sender has been altered. That's because the MIC is a much stronger message verification routine than the ICV.

So should you be encrypting wireless networks with WPA? Not so fast. Data transmitted using WPA encryption was cracked by researchers Erik Tews and Martin Beck in 2008. They attacked the TKIP in order to expose the data. It's not as bad as it sounds. Only the contents of "short" packets were revealed. Others have used the Tews/Beck research to expand the attacks to WPA and reveal more of the encrypted contents.

Just like WEP, there are free tools that can be used to attack WPA encryption. Reaver and aircrack-ng are two such tools. Bottom line . . . don't use WPA either.

WPA2

The next generation of WPA was approved by the IEEE (Institute of Electrical and Electronics Engineers) as 802.11i in 2004. The improvement is called WPA2 (Wi-Fi Protected Access 2) and is also known as Robust Security Network (RSN). The major change in the encryption scheme is that WPA2 uses the AES (Advanced Encryption Standard) block cipher, whereas WEP and WPA use the RC4 stream cipher as described above.

AES is an encryption specification that has been adopted by the U.S. government and is in use worldwide. It is the successor to DES (Data Encryption Standard). The AES specification was approved by the NIST (National Institute of Standards and Technology) in 2001. Like RC4, AES is a symmetric key algorithm, which means the sender and receiver use the same key to encrypt and decrypt the data. A key (no pun intended) difference is that the block size is 128 bits, but there are three key lengths available. You can have a key length of 128, 192, or 256 bits.

The recommendation is to use only WPA2 for encrypting wireless networks. The increased security of the encryption algorithm ensures the confidentiality of the transmitted data. Make sure you check all your wireless devices and verify that they are configured for WPA2 encryption. **If WPA2 is not available for the wireless device, get a replacement device.**

Configuring your wireless access point or wireless router for WPA2 is very simple to do. Access the configuration interface for your wireless router. This is normally done by using a web browser and entering a specific IP address—check your router's instructions for the URL. Navigate to the section that deals with wireless security. You should see something similar to Figure 8.1.

Figure 8.1

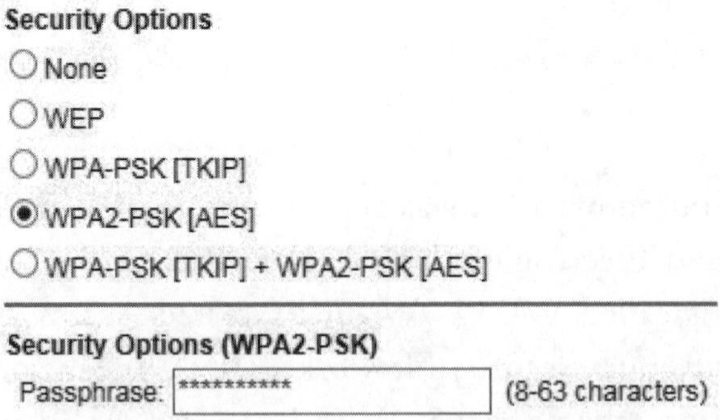

Security Options
○ None
○ WEP
○ WPA-PSK [TKIP]
◉ WPA2-PSK [AES]
○ WPA-PSK [TKIP] + WPA2-PSK [AES]

Security Options (WPA2-PSK)
Passphrase: [**********]   (8-63 characters)

Make the selection for WPA2. You'll also need to enter a passphrase for access to the wireless network. It is a best practice to make this passphrase complex and long, which follows the same recommendations as a login password. You will need to give this passphrase to anyone authorized to access your wireless network.

USING WIRELESS NETWORKS

But how do you tell what type of encryption is being used for the wireless network? Is it WEP, WPA, or WPA2? Can you determine the encryption type prior to connecting? How you access the wireless network properties varies by device and operating system. We won't even attempt to speak to wireless access with a smartphone since there are way too many variants.

If you are using Windows 7, click on the wireless symbol (increasing bars icon to the right of the muted speaker) in the lower right system tray (Figure 8.2).

The available wireless networks will be displayed. Place your mouse over one of the discovered networks and the network properties will be displayed as in Figure 8.3.

Figure 8.2

Figure 8.3

Pay particular attention to the **Security Type** value. As is shown in Figure 8.3, the wireless network named Oak Crest Cloud is encrypted using WPA2. In case you are curious, the PSK or Pre-Shared Key is one of two available authentication methods. PSK is also known as personal mode since it is normally used in home and small business environments. Displaying the network properties prior to connection will let you know if you are about to connect to a potentially insecure wireless network.

If you are running the latest Windows 8.1 version it gets a bit more complicated. When you bring up the list of networks to attach to and put your cursor over the network name, the properties of the network are not shown. Only insecure networks (those with no encryption) will be indicated with an exclamation point on a shield icon as is shown in Figure 8.4. The wireless networks named "ffxlib," "IIP-Print-8A-Officejet Pro 8600," "PUBLIC-PRINT," and "MASON" are networks with no encryption configured. If you attempt to connect to one of them, a message shows that "Other people might be able to see info you send over this network."

Figure 8.4

You can only determine the method of wireless encryption once you are connected to the network. Follow these steps to see the wireless network properties.

1. Swipe from the right edge and select **Settings**

2. Click on or select **Change PC settings**

3. Click on or select **Network**

4. Click on or select the connected wireless network name.

The **Data usage** and **Properties** will be shown for the wireless network. The encryption method will be shown as the **Security type** value. The same problem exists for iOS devices. You cannot determine the encryption type prior to connection. iOS devices will show the encrypted networks with a lock symbol, but you cannot determine which type of encryption is utilized. Insecure wireless networks will not have the lock symbol.

SECURE SOCKET LAYER

You may be familiar with secure socket layer (SSL) connections, but perhaps not familiar with the name of the connection itself. We hope you are familiar with obtaining a secure connection while surfing the Internet. This would be indicated if you use https:// (note the "s," denoting "secure") as part of the URL. Typically, website (http://) connections are unsecured and do not provide an encrypted session as the https:// connections do. SSL connections are not just for websites, although the largest usage is with https connections. You can use SSL over your regular network to encrypt the communication stream as well.

Besides providing a secure encrypted connection to a web server, SSL is used to secure communications to web-based e-mail. Most users will recognize the https:// connection when accessing their e-mail using Outlook Web Access (OWA). These are the two most common uses that users are aware of, but there are a multitude of ways that SSL is used to:

- Secure connection to cloud-based computing platforms for workflow and virtualization applications.
- Secure online credit card transactions.
- Secure transfer of files over https or SFTP (secure FTP).
- Secure the exchange of sensitive information online.
- Secure hosting control panel logins such as cPanel and Parallels.
- Secure web-based e-mail such as Outlook Web Access.
- Secure internal intranet traffic used for file sharing and database connections.
- Secure the connection between the e-mail client and e-mail server such as the connection between Outlook and an Exchange server.
- Secure network logins and network traffic such as SSL VPNs or applications like Citrix.

Secure Socket Layer uses the public-private key encryption system, which also includes the use of a digital certificate. The asymmetric encryption (also known as public-key cryptography) is used for SSL and is considered to be slower than symmetric ciphers such as block or stream ciphers. With this type of encryption, the public key is used to encrypt the data and the private key is used to decrypt the data to render it in a readable form.

For the propeller head readers out there, SSL uses the RSA asymmetric algorithm. RSA is named after its inventors, Ron Rivest, Adi Shamir, and Leonard Adleman. It is the most understood, easiest to implement, and most popular of the asymmetric algorithms. RSA is a worldwide de facto standard that can be used for key exchange, encryption, and digital signatures. It was developed at MIT in 1978 and provides authentication in addition to encryption.

The steps to establishing a SSL connection are listed below.

- The client initiates a connection to the server.
- The server sends the server's certificate to the client.
- The client checks to see if the signing Certificate Authority is in the trusted list for the browser.
- The client computes a hash of the certificate and compares the message digest of the certificate by decrypting using the Certificate Authority's public key.
- The client checks the validity dates in the certificate.
- The client compares the URL listed in the certificate to the URL in the browser before extracting the public key.
- The client extracts the server public key from the certificate.
- The client creates a session key (symmetric).
- The client encrypts the session key with the server's public key and sends it to the server.
- The server decrypts the session key with the server's private key.

As you can see, the certificate plays an important role in securing the communications session. This is why vendors are beginning to reject self-signed certificates and trust only third-party Certificate Authorities. A self-signed certificate is one where you create the certificate yourself and do not use the services of a third-party provider, which provides some level of independent identity validation. It is also possible for a hacker to steal the private key from a digital certificate by infecting the computer with malware. One such example is where hackers broke into an internal server at Adobe to compromise a digital certificate, which allowed them to create at least two files that appeared to be legitimately signed by Adobe. The two files actually contained malware. As a result, Adobe revoked their certificates and reissued new ones. This is a good time to remind you that, when connecting to a secure website, if you're presented with an error message referencing a SSL certificate error or invalid certificate, proceed with extreme caution or, better yet, don't proceed at all.

As final words, the SSL protocol only protects the data for the connection. It does not provide security for the data once it is received. This means that the data is encrypted while it is being transmitted, but once it is received by a computer, the data is no longer encrypted. After all, it has to be in readable form for the recipient. This means you have to trust that the receiving party will take steps to protect the data.

Recent events have uncovered an unfixable flaw in the latest version of SSL. The attack is named POODLE and uncovers a problem with the way SSL 3.0 handles encryption using cipher block mode. It is not important that you understand the technical issues relating to the SSL vulnerability. What's important to know is that you should know how to disable SSL for whatever browser that you use, which is the recommended action. Visit https://zmap.io/sslv3/browsers.html for instructions on how to disable SSL for common browsers. You may be thinking . . . if SSL is dead then how can you have a secure Internet session? The answer is Transport Layer Security (TLS), which is discussed in the next section.

TLS

Transport Layer Security is the successor to SSL and is designed to provide secure communications over the Internet and prevent eavesdropping. The TLS protocol is made up of two layers. The first layer is the TLS Record Protocol, which "rides" on top of TCP (Transport Control Protocol), which is one of the components of Internet traffic. TLS uses symmetric (same key used to encrypt and decrypt) encryption to ensure that the connection is private. It should be noted that the TLS Record Protocol can also be used without encryption. We're not sure why you would do that, but the specification does allow for it. The TLS Record Protocol is also used to encapsulate higher level protocols such as the TLS Handshake Protocol.

The second layer is the TLS Handshake Protocol, which allows authentication between the client and the server. This layer performs the negotiation of the encryption algorithm and cryptographic keys before the transmission or receipt of any data.

TLS is also application protocol independent, which means that higher level protocols can ride on top of TLS. Therefore, TLS provides a secure encrypted network communication facility that any software program can take advantage of. Even though TLS supersedes and extends SSL, it is not interoperable with SSL.

Where do we see TLS used? Many mail systems use TLS to protect the Simple Mail Transfer Protocol (SMTP), which is used to send e-mail messages. In fact, Microsoft's Exchange 2010 has Opportunistic TLS enabled by default. This means that the initial connection tries to use TLS first to secure the communications. You can also enable TLS for older versions of Exchange if you want to send secure e-mail. Besides the default setting for Exchange 2010, Google is now configured to always use TLS-encrypted connections for its Gmail service.

LINK ENCRYPTION

When dealing with encryption of network communications, link encryption can be used to encrypt the communication path. When performing link encryption, all of the data along the communication path is encrypted. This is typically used for connections such as satellite links, telephone circuits, and T3 lines. With link encryption, not only is the user data encrypted, but so are the headers, trailers, addresses, and routing information of the data packets. This gives you an extra layer of protection to help fend off packet sniffers and eavesdroppers.

Link encryption is also known as online encryption and is normally used by service providers in their network protocols. As previously mentioned, all of the information is encrypted and must be decrypted at each hop in the network to determine the next destination. Once the next destination is determined, the packet has to be re-encrypted and sent on its way.

Link encryption is provided by the carrier. While the encryption is normally provided for the carrier's internal usage, you can request that the carrier provide this type of encryption for any service that you may contract for.

END-TO-END ENCRYPTION

Another form of network encryption is end-to-end encryption. With end-to-end encryption, the user data is encrypted, but the routing information (e.g. header, trailer, addresses, etc.) is not encrypted. This means that the various hops in the network do not have to decrypt the routing information in order to determine the next destination. This speeds up the handling of data packets, but also means that hackers can learn more about a captured packet and its destination.

End-to-end encryption usually occurs at the application layer (topmost layer of the OSI model) of the originating computer. It provides more flexibility for the user in determining what data should be encrypted and what should not. It is called end-to-end because the data stays encrypted along its entire journey from the start to the finish.

If you are concerned with someone determining the path or route of the data flow, then you would ask the carrier to provide link encryption as mentioned above. Unless you are dealing with extremely sensitive information and need the security of link encryption to communicate between two parties, end-to-end encryption is usually sufficient.

VIRTUAL PRIVATE NETWORKS (VPN)

Virtual private networks (VPN) are secure connections that typically travel over public networks such as the Internet. The VPN sets up an encrypted tunnel between two points and transmits the data securely through the tunnel. Effectively, it is a point-to-point connection between two devices. VPNs will allow the attorney to access the firm's resources from any location in a secure encrypted fashion. Think of it as extending your private firm network without geographic boundaries. Sort of a virtual network cable without the wires.

VPNs are used for remote access or for connecting two sites. When connecting sites, the VPNs are configured through the router settings at each location. Each router is configured for such values as the remote IP, the method of encryption, type of authentication, etc. Many home and small business routers have the ability to create a

VPN tunnel between two locations. Setting up the VPN can be a little confusing for some and may require the assistance of your IT provider.

Many attorneys will be familiar with using a VPN for remote access to the firm's computing resources. You need to configure a VPN server for the host (e.g. law firm server) and then each remote computer needs to have VPN client software. Cisco's VPN software is very commonly used, especially since Cisco routers are also prevalent in law firm networks. However, Cisco is not the only vendor that provides VPN software. There are free open source VPN software products and VPN is even built into the Windows operating system. Finally, you can subscribe to a VPN service for a monthly fee where they provide the software to load on your computer. VPN services from Comodo and LogMeIn Hamachi are popular third-party providers of VPN services.

It is fairly easy to set up a VPN if you are using Windows 7. The simplest way to get started is to click the Start button and type in **VPN** in the search box. This will return a **Set up a virtual private network (VPN) connection** selection. Once you have launched the wizard for setting up the VPN continue with the following steps:

1. In the **Internet Address** field enter the IP address or the host name (e.g. vpn.myoffice.com). This value is normally obtained from your network administrator. Typically it's the public IP address of your router.

2. You can change the **Destination name** field to indicate something more descriptive about the connection. Perhaps entering something like *VPN to Smith, Apple and Green, PLC* would be a better choice when naming the connection.

3. Check the box **Don't connect now; just set it up so I can connect later.** This will save the settings for future use.

4. Click the **Next** button.

5. The next dialog box is for the logon credentials. If you leave the **User name** and **Password** blank, you will be prompted for them when the connection is attempted. If you are connecting to your firm's network, it is suggested that you fill in the **Domain (optional)** value. The recommendation is to leave the **User name** and **Password** blank.

6. Click the **Create** button.

That's it. When you are ready to connect, just click on the network icon in the system tray. The networks available for connection will be listed. Select the VPN network you previously configured.

Figure 8.5

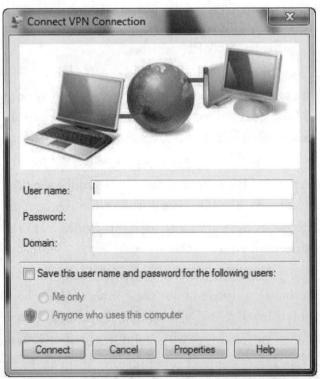

The VPN connection box (Figure 8.5) will be displayed. Fill in the appropriate logon information and click the **Connect** button. If the connection fails, click the **Properties** button. The most common failure is the type of VPN setting. Normally, you would leave this set to **Automatic**. Check with the network administrator to see if it should be set to PPTP, L2TP/IPSec, SSTP, or IKEv2.

VPN setup gets a little more complicated with Windows 8 and 8.1 systems. The step are similar to a Windows 7 environment, but how you get to the various data entry fields is different. It is best to get your IT support personnel to setup the VPN for you. If you are really brave, just Google "how to configure vpn in windows 8.1" and you'll get lots of suggestions.

RDP

Another secure network communication method is Remote Desktop Protocol (RDP). RDP is another built-in feature of Windows and is similar to the VPN connection previously described. RDP is an encrypted network connection that is similar to a VPN. A VPN sets up a secure encrypted connection as if it were an encrypted "wire" back to the office network, whereas a RDP connection is more than just a connection. The RDP session is actually similar to a remote control scenario like GoToMyPC or LogMeIn. By using Windows RDP you are creating a desktop connection to the remote site. The computer you are connecting to has to have RDP sessions enabled in order to accept the inbound connection. To establish a RDP session, just click on the **Remote Desktop Connection** icon in the Accessories folder on a Windows system. Just enter the IP address or host name and click the **Connect** button. Enter your login credentials for authentication and the RDP session will be established.

You will probably need assistance from your IT provider to initially enable RDP and make sure that you have a fixed IP address to connect to. Dynamic IP addresses are typically used for home network connections and are not acceptable for RDP or VPN connections. A static IP address is needed so that you always connect to the same address. You wouldn't know where to connect if the address changes as it does with dynamic IPs.

SUMMARY

We've discussed several methods to securely communicate over a network. When using wireless networks, WPA2 is the recommended encryption method. Now that SSL is effectively dead, TLS is really your only choice for secure network communications, especially when using your browser. Finally, encrypted remote sessions can be achieved using VPNs or RDP sessions.

Chapter 9
ELECTRONIC COMMUNICATIONS

This chapter will deal with how attorneys secure electronic communications. The most used method of electronically communicating today is via e-mail. Some may argue that text messaging is the number one method and that may be true for the younger generation, but businesses are generally communicating with some sort of e-mail service. The issue that we need to tackle is whether our electronic communications are secure (or need to be) and how to securely communicate when needed.

As we have mentioned previously, attorneys have an ethical duty to protect the confidentiality of client information. It's not just the written word and paper documents. The duty extends to electronic communications as well. Sending a simple e-mail message potentially exposes the contents to interception by the bad guys if not our own government. Encryption can protect the electronic communications thereby preserving the confidentiality of the information. In addition, digitally signing communications helps ensure the authenticity of the sender.

Many security professionals describe the sending of unencrypted e-mail as the electronic version of a postcard, where the data is easy to read. Encrypting the communications is similar to putting the contents into a sealed envelope and sending it on its way. Nobody will be able to read the contents, unlike an unencrypted message.

MICROSOFT EXCHANGE SERVER

By default, Exchange is configured automatically to attempt to communicate with other servers using TLS (Transport Layer Security), which is covered in more detail in the previous chapter. This means that communications between servers travel in an encrypted state. You can also configure Exchange so that communications between two domains is required to be encrypted using TLS. If the same encryption level does not exist between the two domains (for example, between mylawfirm.com and myfirmclient.com), the messages are returned and a non-delivery report (NDR) is generated. Obviously, this would be a very secure configuration and something that may be considered for use between the firm and specific clients. However, implementing such configurations is best left to the technology professionals. We are pretty sure we won't see very many attorneys attempting to do this on their own.

Exchange can also be configured to require TLS encryption for the accessing computers. This means that any software (e.g., Outlook) must use TLS in order to access a mailbox. Again, your IT person is probably better equipped to configure the TLS requirement for client computers.

OUTLOOK WEB ACCESS

Many users of Microsoft Exchange know that they can access their mailboxes using a browser instead of Outlook. Browser access is good when you don't have your laptop or other mobile device available. Typically you may be using Outlook Web Access (OWA) when visiting at another office, on vacation at an Internet café, or using a hotel business center. Using OWA on public computers can be a real security risk. Recently, the U.S. Secret Service in collaboration with the National Cybersecurity and Communications Integration Center (NCCIC) issued a warning that hotel business center computers are being targeted by hackers.[1] Keylogger malware is being installed at an increasing rate on these public computers, presumably with the intent of stealing personally identifiable information (PII).

Configuring OWA to use SSL/TLS will encrypt the transmission of the information from your computer to the Exchange server. You enable SSL on the OWA Exchange Server virtual directory to enable this feature. The Directory Security should also be configured to "Require Secure Channel when accessing this resource," which will ensure that OWA always uses SSL/TLS to communicate. Just remember that using SSL/TLS will not protect you if keylogger software is installed on the computer you are using. The keystroke logging software will capture everything you type BEFORE it is transmitted over the SSL/TLS connection.

OUTLOOK/EXCHANGE

Similar to configuring OWA for secure access, you should configure Outlook to connect securely to Exchange as well. Most attorneys are using Outlook to access their mailboxes, calendars, tasks, contacts, etc. Make sure that you are configured to encrypt the data between Outlook and the Exchange server. If you are using Outlook 2010 or 2013, confirm the setting by following the steps below:

1. Select the **File** tab in the Ribbon
2. Click on the **Account Settings** icon and select Account Settings
3. Select the e-mail address under the **Mail** tab
4. Click on **Change . . .** in the menu choice

---

1   ZDNet, "US Secret Service warns of keyloggers on public hotel computers," Last modified July 14, 2014, http://www.zdnet.com/us-secret-service-warns-of-keyloggers-on-public-hotel-computers-7000031557.

5. Click on the **More Settings . . .** button

6. Click on the **Security** tab

7. Make sure that the checkbox is selected as in Figure 9.1

Figure 9.1

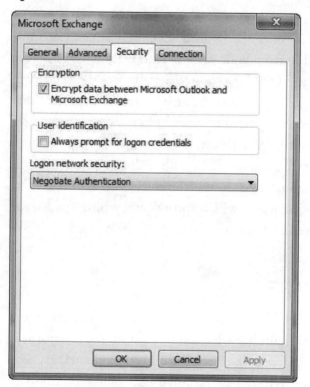

This security option has been enabled by default since Outlook 2007 and is used when the Outlook client is on the same network as the Exchange server. Exchange Server 2003 introduced the remote procedure call (RPC) over HTTPS feature, which is a secure way to communicate with Exchange. Outlook 2003 and later and Exchange 2003 and later support the use of RPC over HTTPS. You should recognize HTTPS as being a secure encrypted form of communication. By using RPC over HTTPS, users no longer have to use a virtual private network (VPN) connection or the "Encrypt data between Microsoft Outlook and Microsoft Exchange" setting to securely access their mailbox. The MAPI/RPC connection is established by tunneling RPC traffic over HTTPS.

GMAIL

Many attorneys use Google's e-mail service for their practice. Google is currently in the process of modifying all of its services to provide encryption by default. Documents disclosed by Edward Snowden reported that the NSA had tapped the undersea fiber optic cable that runs between two of Google's data centers. The data moving over the fiber was in clear text and being intercepted by the NSA. Ever since then, Google has been moving on a forced march pace to encrypt all of the communications and services it provides.

You may know that search results are now being encrypted by Google. Just do a normal Google search. Notice that the URL automatically switches to https:// and the returned results are encrypted. Google is doing this to protect the privacy of the returned information. Besides search results, Google is forcing https:// connections to Gmail. This will encrypt the communications between your computer and Google's servers. In addition, the default is for Google to use TLS (see the previous chapter) for server to server communication.

In June of 2014, Google announced a new tool called End-to-End. It's a Chrome browser extension that will keep the data encrypted until the recipient decrypts it. An extension is software that provides additional function for the browser. The code is available to those technically inclined and uses OpenPGP (Open source encryption software). Once the Chrome extension is tested and ready for prime-time, Google will make it available in the Chrome Web Store.

E-MAIL ENCRYPTION

This topic can be complicated and confusing for most lawyers. Up to this point, we have discussed ways to encrypt the traffic from Outlook to the Exchange server and the communications between servers. But what if you only need to encrypt a single message? The data flow is the same as if you were encrypting a file. Instead the "file" is an e-mail message.

Figure 9.2 Encrypted E-mail

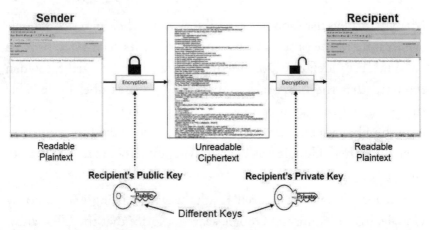

Figure 9.2 shows the steps (in simplistic form) for encrypting a single message. The sender starts by composing the e-mail message in plaintext. When the message is transmitted, the recipient's public key is used to encrypt the message with the output being unreadable ciphertext. The ciphertext (encrypted data) is sent along its merry way destined for the recipient. The recipient then uses the private key to decrypt the ciphertext into readable plaintext.

As you can see, it is extremely important for the sender to have a copy of the recipient's public key in order to make this work. Key exchange and management are some of the challenges when trying to encrypt e-mail messages. Since the recipient is the only one with the private key (he or she better be the only one) that is used in decrypting the data, confidentiality is maintained.

You can also digitally sign a message to maintain the authenticity of the sender. In those cases, the message is encrypted with the sender's private key and the recipient decrypts it with the sender's public key. There is no confidentiality of the message when it is digitally signed. This is because the sender's public key is public and can be decrypted by anyone.

Digital signature services provide integrity, authentication, and nonrepudiation. A hash function is used to facilitate the digital signature services. A hash value (or just hash) is also called a message digest. When you hash data or in this case a message, a formula is applied to the data that produces a substantially smaller value in such a way that it is extremely unlikely that any other text would produce the same value. Common hash algorithms are MD5, SHA-1, and SHA-256. When you digitally sign a message, a hash of the message is obtained and then encrypted with the sender's private key. The result is sent along with the original message. Upon receipt, the recipient removes the encrypted hash from the original message and decrypts the hash with the sender's public key. The recipient then hashes the original message and compares it to the hash that was sent with the message. If both hash values match then we know that the message was not modified in transit, therefore the integrity of the message was maintained. In addition, the authenticity of the sender is verified through the use of the sender's private and public keys. A simple representation is shown in Figure 9.3.

Figure 9.3 Signed E-Mail

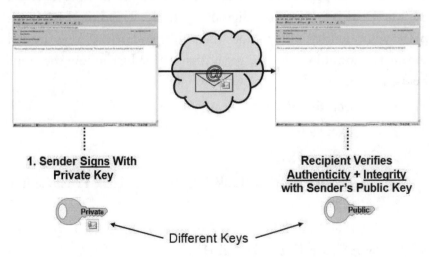

1. Sender <u>Signs</u> With Private Key

Recipient Verifies <u>Authenticity</u> + <u>Integrity</u> with Sender's Public Key

Different Keys

When you send an encrypted message, you can also digitally sign it at the same time. As previously mentioned, the recipient's public and private keys are used for the encryption process. Figure 9.4 is a simple representation of encrypting and signing a message at the same time.

Figure 9.4 Encrypted and Signed E-Mail

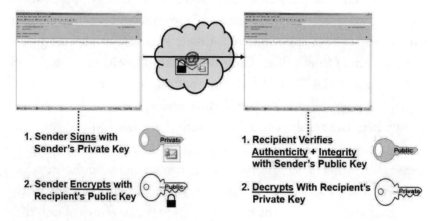

1. Sender <u>Signs</u> with Sender's Private Key

2. Sender <u>Encrypts</u> with Recipient's Public Key

1. Recipient Verifies <u>Authenticity</u> + <u>Integrity</u> with Sender's Public Key

2. <u>Decrypts</u> With Recipient's Private Key

OUTLOOK MESSAGES

Now we'll describe the requirements and steps to encrypt a message when using Outlook. As previously stated, the majority of attorneys use Outlook as their e-mail client. The first requirement is to have a digital ID, also known as a digital certificate. The digital ID helps prove your identity and includes the public and private keys needed for encryption. How do you get a digital ID? Just follow the steps below from Outlook:

1. Click on the **File** tab

2. Click **Options**

3. Click **Trust Center**

4. Under **Microsoft Outlook Trust Center**, click **Trust Center Settings ...**

5. On the **E-mail Security** tab, under **Digital IDs (Certificates)**, click **Get a Digital ID ...**

Figure 9.5

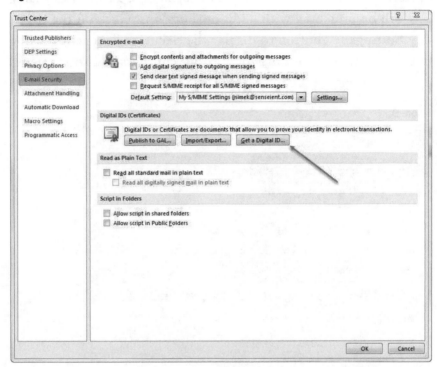

You will then open a browser window where you will have a choice to select a digital ID provider. Once you have selected a provider and obtained your digital ID, follow the provider's instructions on how to install the digital certificate to your computer.

Once you have installed your digital ID, you can begin the process of sending an encrypted message from Outlook. Create your message and include any attachments you want to send along. Once you are ready to send the message, select the **Options** tab from the ribbon and then the **More Options** symbol as shown by the arrow in Figure 9.6.

Figure 9.6

After selecting the **More Options** symbol, a **Properties** dialog box will be presented with additional options. Click on the **Security Settings** ... button to display the **Security Properties** dialog box. Check the box for **Encrypt message contents and attachments** as shown in Figure 9.7 to encrypt the e-mail.

Figure 9.7

You can also digitally sign the message by selecting the **Add digital signature to this message** option. Once your selections are completed, just send the message. If you see a dialog box like the one in Figure 9.8, there is either a missing or invalid certificate for the recipient(s).

Figure 9.8

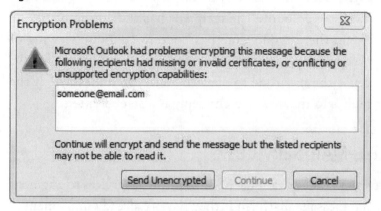

Remember we said previously that you need the public key of the recipient(s) in order to encrypt the message? If there is a problem with the certificate, therefore the key, you have the option of sending the message unencrypted by just clicking the **Send Unencrypted** button. Bottom line . . . you'll need to get a valid certificate for the recipient if you want to send encrypted communications.

OFFICE 365 MESSAGE ENCRYPTION

Many attorneys are using the subscription-based Office 365 offering from Microsoft in their practices. Encrypting messages using Office 365 is very easy to accomplish. You create a policy on the server by defining transport rules that determine the conditions for encryption. As an example, the rule can require that all communications to a specific recipient be encrypted.

When a user sends a message that matches the encryption rule, it is sent out with a HTML attachment. The recipient clicks on the attachment, which opens a browser and prompts the user to login with a free Microsoft account. Some recipients don't have (and don't want) a Microsoft account. The recipient has the option of having Microsoft send them a one-time passcode to facilitate viewing of the encrypted message instead of logging on. The recipient has 15 minutes to use the passcode to view the encrypted message. If the recipient replies to the message, the reply is also encrypted.

SECURE E-MAIL SERVICES

Many attorneys take advantage of secure e-mail services to augment their normal message platform if they haven't already implemented a complete secure messaging infrastructure. A common approach is to access a secure portal to retrieve messages. This process is shown in Figure 9.9 and is also known as "pull" e-mail.

Figure 9.9 Pull E-mail

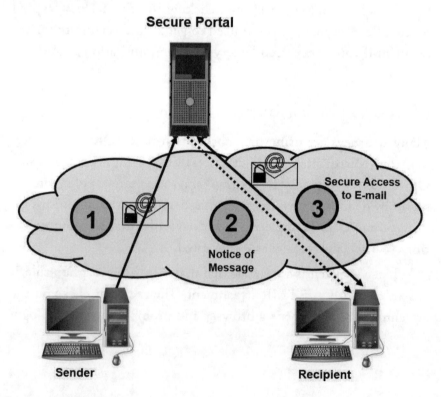

In the pull scenario, a secure message is sent using the provider's service. This could be a gateway appliance installed on your own network, configuration of your outbound mail routing, or just using a browser to access the service. Once the message is at the secure e-mail provider, a notification is sent to the recipient that there is a message. Typically, the notice includes a link so the recipient can quickly access the message. The recipient connects to the secure portal and then "pulls" the message for reading.

There is also a "push" method of delivery. When communicating in this fashion, the message is sent as an encrypted attachment to a normal e-mail. The recipient then decrypts the attachment to view the contents. With this type of delivery, no login to the service provider is required.

Figure 9.10 Push E-mail

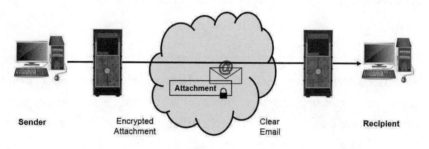

| Sender | Encrypted Attachment | Clear Email | Recipient |

There are many providers of secure e-mail. Just do a Google search and all sorts of results will be returned. How do they work and what features are important? We can't possibly cover all the solutions. ProtonMail (https://protonmail.ch/) gets high marks and good reviews. It is a complete end-to-end encrypted messaging system that does not require any installation. Other highly rated providers include 4SecureMail.com, ShazzleMail.com, and Start-Mail.com. See if the vendor offers a trial period and if their system can integrate in your current e-mail environment with ease.

HUSHMAIL

It would be impossible to discuss all the possible options for sending encrypted communications. One very popular service is called Hushmail. They have plans for individuals, businesses, and HIPAA compliance. Hushmail is a web-based e-mail service that provides encrypted communications between parties. While Hushmail encrypts e-mail, it is not a totally secure solution. The servers are located in British Columbia, Canada, and the company will comply with any lawful request to access the data. Under normal circumstances they do not store the passphrase that is used for encryption/decryption. However, it may be required to store a passphrase for an account identified in an order enforceable in British Columbia, Canada. Like the encrypted services of some cloud-storage vendors, you need to understand that Hushmail does have the ability to access messages even though they are encrypted.

ZIXCORP

Another service that is worth considering is the e-mail encryption service of Zix Corportation. ZixCorp is the only e-mail encryption provider with SOC3/SysTrust certification, SOC2 accreditation, and PCI Level 1, DSS V2.0 certification. Suffice it to say that Zix is a very robust solution that meets the security requirements of many industries. The encryption service is easy to install and very simple to use.

Most attorneys will subscribe to the ZixCorp service through a reseller. The reseller will set up the outbound mail flow so that messages are routed through the ZixCorp servers. This is a similar configuration to many spam and antivirus services. The user installs an Outlook add-in that provides for one-button-click encryption. Compose your message and just click the button (Figure 9.11) to **Encrypt & Send**. Simple, right? The message is then sent to the ZixCorp servers.

Figure 9.11

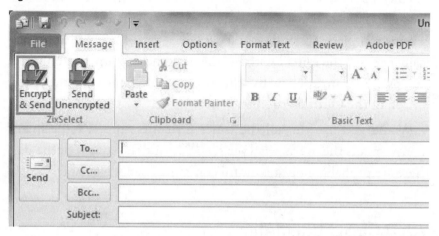

If the recipients can receive messages via a TLS connection, the message is delivered to directly to their inbox and is opened in Outlook with no further processing. If they do not have the ability to receive e-mail via TLS, they receive a link to the message on the ZixCorp servers. The recipients will have to create a login ID or login to their account if they have already created one. They then retrieve the message. In other words, a non-TLS enabled user will be viewing the decrypted messages via a web browser once he or she has logged in. It couldn't be easier.

If the message is delivered directly to the recipient's inbox, the recipient knows that the message was secured throughout its journey by the insertion of the ZixCorp graphic at the end of the message as in Figure 9.12. This footer message is inserted by Zix for the e-mail that is delivered via a TLS connection. In addition, you have the option to set policies where the messages will automatically get encrypted based on message content. As an example, you can have a

Figure 9.12

This message was secured by ZixCorp.
To reach ZixCorp, go to: http://www.zixcorp.com/info/zixmail

This message was secured by ZixCorp(R).

"financial policy," where Zix scans the e-mail for the inclusion of any financial data such as bank account numbers, credit card numbers, routing numbers, etc. If financial data exists, then Zix will automatically encrypt the e-mail without the user clicking any buttons. You can override any policy by clicking on the **Send Unencrypted** button in the Outlook toolbar.

Would you use this all the time? Of course not. Of the many, many e-mails the average lawyer sends during the course of the day, there are probably only a handful containing sensitive data.

VOLTAGE SECUREMAIL

Like ZixCorp, Voltage is a secure message delivery system. Voltage SecureMail provides end-to-end security for e-mail and attachments. Their service is similar to ZixCorp and can be deployed throughout the enterprise. The solution reaches from the desktop through the enterprise and out to mobile devices. SecureMail integrates with pretty much everything at the firm including Outlook, mail hygiene, data loss prevention (DLP), archive and e-discovery, Blackberry Enterprise Server, and mobile device management (MDM). Integration with Active Directory is a big benefit for those firms running Windows domain environments.

You can deploy SecureMail on-premises (larger firms) or use the cloud solution called Voltage SecureMail Cloud. SecureMail is available in three main editions. The Essentials Edition provides encryption and decryption at the network edge via policies or can be activated by using a "Send Secure" button within Outlook. The Standard Edition builds on the Essentials Edition and provides encryption internally within the firm. The Enterprise Edition includes all the features of Standard plus the ability to encrypt files and documents.

MIMECAST

Mimecast is a hosted (cloud) secure e-mail service that is popular with mid-sized and large law firms. It has several security features, including encryption. Its encryption options include enforced gateway-to-gateway encryption (e.g., between a law firm's e-mail server and client e-mail servers), secure e-mail delivery to third parties, and end-user controlled encryption.

PHONE CALLS AND TEXT

By default, cellular communications (e.g. voice and text) are encrypted between your device and the cellular provider, but the carrier determines the encryption method. Since the carriers control the encryption, they have the ability to decode the communications and have done so in aiding law enforcement investigations. So how can you maintain your privacy and keep your telephone calls and text messages secure from prying eyes? You can always purchase the Blackphone (https://blackphone.ch) by Silent Circle and Geeksphone to make secure encrypted phone calls, secure browsing, secure file transfer, secure video, secure text, etc. The phone is specifically designed to optimize privacy. It is built from the ground up to be secure by design. It costs $629 and is available for North America (Region 2) and Rest of World (Region 1).

While the Blackphone is a device specifically designed for secure communications, we don't think most lawyers will pony up the money or need a device that has security elevated to such a high level. We would suggest that lawyers use a product like RedPhone for their Android device. RedPhone is free and provides end-to-end encryption for your calls. This means your conversations are secure so nobody can listen in. It does mean that the recipient must also have RedPhone installed. You use the phone just like you normally would, but you have the opportunity to upgrade to an encrypted call if the contact is also a RedPhone user. You can even keep your same phone number. Products like RedPhone would certainly be a first step towards secure encrypted communications, especially since it's free.

But what about text messages? The makers of RedPhone (Open Whisper Systems) also have a free product for sending encrypted text messages called TextSecure. TextSecure is a replacement for the default text messaging application. The text messages are encrypted locally so they are not accessible if your phone is lost. In addition, the text messages are encrypted when sent between TextSecure users.

SKYPE

We used to tell attorneys that it was acceptable to use Skype for confidential conversations. Skype is a peer-to-peer encrypted voice and video communications environment. The peer-to-peer nature of the communications made the communications near impossible to trace since you didn't know which computers were handling which packets of data for the call. Even if you did, the data packets are encrypted.

Well, all of that has changed. Microsoft now owns Skype. Over the last several years, Microsoft has been changing the architecture of the Skype network and all traffic now routes through Microsoft controlled servers. Technology site Ars technica performed a test and caught Microsoft accessing the content of the messages.[2] In addition, Edward Snowden released documents revealing that

---

2   Ars Technica, "Think your Skype messages get end-to-end encryption? Think again," Last modified May 20, 2013, http://arstechnica.com/security/2013/05/think-your-skype-messages-get-end-to-end-encryption-think-again/.

Microsoft cooperated with the NSA in the PRISM project to decrypt the Skype conversations.[3] So much for end-to-end encryption.

This is the same situation we discuss concerning cloud providers. Access to your data is still at risk if the vendor has access to the decryption key. Since Microsoft can decrypt the Skype data and the user doesn't define the encryption key, attorneys should use caution when using Skype for confidential information and consider avoiding it for highly sensitive information.

VIDEO CONFERENCING

Most commentators feel that it is safe to use the services of any major video conference provider. GoToMeeting by Citrix and Cisco's WebEx are examples of trusted providers. Like other communications streams, the video conferencing data packets are encrypted in transit. However, there is still the possibility that the data stream can be captured and decrypted since it flows through the vendor's servers similar to the Skype network.

There are bigger things to worry about than a vendor accessing your video conferencing sessions. How about not locking down access to participate or viewing saved conferences? Security expert Brian Krebs identified several companies that hold recurring meetings and don't password protect access.[4] The companies included Charles Schwab, CSC, CBS, CVS, U.S. Department of Energy, Fannie Mae, Jones Day, Orbitz, Paychex Services, and Union Pacific.

---

3 *International Business Times*, "Snowden Reveals Microsoft PRISM Cooperation: Helped NSA Decrypt Emails, Chats, Skype Conversations," Last modified July 11, 2013, http://www.ibtimes.com/snowden-reveals-microsoft-prism-cooperation-helped-nsa-decrypt-emails-chats-skype-conversations.

4 KrebsOnSecurity, "Who's Watching Your WebEx?" Last modified October 14, 2014, https://krebsonsecurity.com/2014/10/whos-watching-your-webex/.

Notice the law firm name? In response, Cisco posted six easy ways to protect WebEx meetings.[5]

1. Make your meeting unlisted
2. Require a complex password
3. Choose meeting information carefully
4. Disable "join before host"
5. Set "Host as presenter"
6. Learn about other best practices

We've heard of other firms that leave their video conference equipment set to auto-answer. Not a good idea either. Sometimes it doesn't take encryption to protect communications. Some common sense helps too.

PRACTICAL STEPS

As you can see, there are many options for encrypting your electronic communications. Encrypting e-mail is getting easier and easier through the use of services such as Zix. Apps for your smartphone also make encrypting communications as simple as just making a call using the app's dialer. Encrypting messages using digital certificates is a little more complicated, but certainly easy enough for most lawyers to implement. The good news is that many of the options are not very expensive and can serve the solo and small firm lawyer as well as the large firm attorney.

---

5   Cisco WebEx, "Protecting Your WebEx Meeting Information," http://blog.webex.com/2014/10/protecting-webex-meeting-information, last visited October 14, 2014.

Chapter 10

It seems like everybody is talking about "the cloud" and what new uses it provides for lawyers and law firms. All this talk got us thinking about how little the typical lawyer knows about cloud services. Many attorneys can't really even describe what "the cloud" is. You would be amazed at how many lawyers think "the cloud" is somehow impacted by the weather. We can't really blame them—the definitions for "the cloud" are all over the place. Our focus here is security of data held by a cloud-service provider and data in transit between an attorney or law firm and a cloud service provider.

Generally, services that are provided in the cloud are provisioned by technology that is not physically located in your office. In other words, it is remote and off-premises. You can certainly own the equipment yourself and house it at a data center with everything under your control. There are a lot of other options for cloud computing as well. You could purchase computing "space" on equipment owned and/or operated by someone else. Think of Amazon's Web Services, where Amazon owns the hardware and network and you purchase computing capacity and storage from them. Finally, you can purchase application access from the vendor, where it provides all the equipment, network, data center, and the application software too. Think of Google Docs, where you can create documents on Google's hardware via an Internet connection.

Probably the first place that lawyers go for cloud services is off-site storage. According to the ABA 2014 *Legal Technology Survey Report*, 56 percent of respondents reported using online storage for law-related tasks. The explosion of iPad usage drove hordes of lawyers to Dropbox. Dropbox is the 800-pound gorilla of cloud storage. It seems that software developers provide integration with Dropbox storage before any other cloud provider. However, the tide is starting to shift and other providers like Box, OneDrive, and Google Drive are taking part of the market share from Dropbox. Security is a major concern for attorneys and more scrutiny is being placed upon the cloud providers, especially storage providers.

In addition to storage providers, cloud-based case management applications are very popular. Document management is also growing in popularity as lawyers look for ways to reduce their expenses and increase productivity. Clio is one of the most popular cloud-based case management applications. Other options for case management include Rocket Matter and Houdini, Esq. NetDocuments owns the beachhead for cloud-document assembly, but the cloud offering from Worldox is gaining market share as an alternative to their on premise solution.

We can't cover all of the options for cloud services, but we'll try to run through some of the more popular ones for attorneys. As the book title indicates, we are concerned with services that provide some level of encryption as a protection mechanism. Not all providers are created equal and encryption capabilities vary. It is important for attorneys to understand how their client data is being protected. Sometimes the lawyer will have to implement additional technologies or configuration to increase the default protections of the cloud provider. Hopefully, we can explain the pros and cons of the service providers and any additional steps you may have to take to protect client confidentiality.

Confidential data should be encrypted when it is stored in the cloud. An important consideration for security of encrypted data in storage is who controls the decryption key. Encryption controlled by the end-user can protect the confidentiality of the data since the encryption key is only known to the creator of the data. Figure 10.1 shows the difference with control of the key by the end-user and control by the service provider. If the end-user controls the key, the data is protected everywhere it resides away from the end-user. Confidentiality does not depend on the effectiveness of the security of the cloud service provider.

Figure 10.1

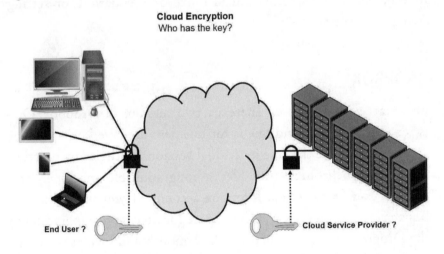

Consensus security standards for cloud services are still developing. There is not an absolute requirement that encryption must be controlled by the end-user, but it should be the default. End-user control of encryption should be required unless the end-user makes an informed decision that the data is not sensitive enough to require this level of protection or that the cloud service provider will implement and maintain sufficient security controls without end-user encryption. For attorneys, this requires the analysis required by the ethics rules and opinions discussed in Chapter 2. It requires competent and reasonable measures to safeguard information relating to clients, due diligence concerning service providers, and requiring service providers to safeguard data in accordance with attorneys' confidentiality obligations.

It is also important to make sure the data is transferred to the cloud provider over a secure encrypted connection such as https:// and that the cloud provider implements strong encryption for data at rest. Finally, no system is secure if you use weak login credentials. You should be using a strong password or passphrase (complexity and length) for authentication and enable two factor authentication if available. See Chapters 5 and 11 for recommendations on setting strong passwords.

DROPBOX

Let's start with Dropbox. There are two versions of Dropbox. One is for individual use and one is for business use. We know a lot of attorneys that use the free individual version for their law practice. Dropbox synchronizes the files among multiple machines and devices. You first create a Dropbox account. If you select the free basic package, you get two GB of space for no charge. Upgrading to the Dropbox Pro account costs $9.99/month and increases storage to one TB (1,000 GB) of space. Make sure that you also enable two-factor authentication to make access to your account more secure.

But should an attorney use Dropbox? That depends. Dropbox does transfer the data to its servers using SSL so you know it's encrypted in transmission. They also encrypt your data while at rest. However, they have access to the decryption keys and the ability to access user data. The Dropbox website states, "Dropbox employees are prohibited from viewing the content of files you store in your account." To further support the fact that Dropbox can access user data the Help Center states, "Like most online services, we have a small number of employees who must be able to access user data for the reasons stated in our privacy policy (e.g., when legally required to do so)." Not a good thing if you are trying to keep your client's data confidential.

There was also an event in June of 2011 that was called the "Dropbox Password Debacle" by many commentators. Dropbox implemented some programming updates to their system over a weekend. The result of the update was to break the password authentication system for all Dropbox users. This meant that anyone could login to a Dropbox account with an incorrect or no password for about four hours on a Sunday. So much for security. Good luck if you had confidential data stored on Dropbox since it was exposed to the public for the entire period. There may not have been reports of data being compromised, but that's not surprising. We don't hear of many law firm data breaches either.

So what does all this mean? **Dropbox should not be used for any confidential information unless you encrypt the data before sending it to Dropbox.** We'll cover some ways to do that below, but realize that the standard way of using Dropbox employed by most attorneys makes it suitable only for storing data that does not require encryption to protect it. However, you can password protect documents to encrypt the contents, which is covered in Chapter 11. The authors regularly use Dropbox to share data that is not confidential such as CLE materials and PowerPoint presentations.

It should be noted that Dropbox does have a business offering, which has additional features for the enterprise environment. Audit logs, device management, two-factor authentication, single sign-on, file recovery, and remote wipe are just some of the additional features in the Dropbox for Business offering. As Dropbox continues to evolve its business offerings, it may reach the point where it is an option for confidential data.

BOX

Another highly rated cloud-storage (and sharing) service is Box. Box is similar to Dropbox, but is geared more to the business community with different levels of features. You can control access to the data in a very granular fashion with an administrative console, where you set user access along with content policies and automations to create simple workflows. They do have a personal plan with ten GB of free storage that can also synchronize across multiple devices. Data is transmitted over an encrypted SSL connection and protected at rest with 256-bit AES encryption.

Just like Dropbox, Box has access to your content. Specifically, Box states that it needs access to your content in order to "(a) comply with the law or respond to lawful requests or legal process; (b) protect the rights or property of Box or our customers, including the enforcement of our agreements or policies governing your use of the Service; or (c) act on a good faith belief that such access or disclosure is necessary to protect the personal safety of Box employees, customers, or the public." This means Box has access to the encryption keys and can decrypt the data as it sees fit, subject to its terms of service.

A number of businesses, including law firms, have announced that they are using Box for Business. While it does not currently offer end-user encryption, it does have a number of security features that allow the end-user's IT staff to control access and use and provides for monitoring and auditing of users. Box has announced that it is working on providing end-user control of encryption for its business offerings, but it is not currently available.

MORE FILE SYNCHRONIZATION AND SHARING OPTIONS

We can't cover all of the options for secure file synchronization and sharing in a short book focusing on encryption, but there are three more, with high ratings in reviews, that we want to cover briefly. They are used by a number of mid-sized and large law firms. They are Accellion (http://accellion.com), Citrix ShareFile (http://www.share file.com), and EMC Syncplicity (http://www.emc.com/storage/online-file-sharing-enterprise.htm#). Accellion's file synchronization and sharing product is fully on-premises, so it is administered by a law firm's IT staff, giving the law firm complete control over the data. Citrix provides options that include on-premises, managed cloud, and hybrid with elements of both. Syncplicity also offers on-premises and hosted cloud options. Because the offerings keep developing and changing, it is best to consult current reviews and check with law firms that use these kinds of services when selecting an option.

SPIDEROAK

By now you should see how important it is for the user to control the encryption key. Your data can potentially be accessed by others if the vendor has the encryption key. The only real way to protect the confidentiality of the information is when the user has control and defines the encryption passphrase. SpiderOak is a service that is designed for privacy. It has no access to the plaintext version of any data that is uploaded to its servers. The service is marketed as a backup solution, but you can also share data.

SpiderOak has a "Zero-Knowledge" privacy guarantee. Since everything is encrypted throughout the process, the staff at SpiderOak cannot even know the names of your files or folders. All the SpiderOak staff can see are sequentially numbered containers of encrypted data. The first time you run the SpiderOak software on a computer, a series of strong encryption keys are generated. The keys are themselves encrypted with your password and stored (along with your backup data) on SpiderOak servers in their encrypted form. This is no doubt why so many journalists use SpiderOak.

Sign up for your free account at https://spideroak.com. Enter your name, e-mail address, user name, and password. SpiderOak encrypts everything, including all transmissions to its servers. As a result, some password managers (1Pass, LastPass, KeePass, Keychain) won't work with SpiderOak. That's because the password managers track what is transmitted to the service and not what the user types into the password field. Since SpiderOak encrypts the password prior to sending, the password manager is incorrectly saving the encrypted hash of the password instead of the password itself. Your password is not stored or known to SpiderOak. Once you create your account, you will be prompted to install the SpiderOak application to your computer.

You then configure what data you want to back up to the SpiderOak servers. The basic setup allows you to select categories or groupings. Those would include Desktop, Documents, Favorites, Movies, Music, and Pictures. Selecting the categories doesn't really show you what specific files will be uploaded. Selecting the advanced button allows you to select any file or folder on your computer.

SpiderOak is really serious about its encryption implementation. It uses a variety of different methods to make sure that your data is kept private and only accessible to you. It uses 256-bit AES encryption in cipher feedback (CFB) mode. CFB describes the steps that are taken in order to encrypt the plaintext. Basically the ciphertext from one block is used to encrypt the plaintext in the next block. Then it becomes a "wash, rinse, repeat" cycle, with the resulting ciphertext being used to encrypt the next plaintext block and it goes on and on until the data is fully encrypted.

Besides using AES-256, SpiderOak uses a nested series of key scopes, which means there is a new encryption key for each folder, version of a file and the individual data blocks that compose a file version. This method enables the effective sharing of selected portions of data while keeping the rest private. Another key feature is that the keys are never stored in plaintext on the SpiderOaks servers. The keys themselves are encrypted using 256-bit AES encryption using a key created from the user's password by the key derivation/strengthening algorithm of Password-Based Key Derivation Function 2 (PBKDF2) with a minimum of 16,384 rounds and 32 bytes (not bits) of random data. The original specification for PBKDF2 recommended a minimum of 1,000 rounds. The approach used by SpiderOak prevents brute force and pre-computation or database attacks against the key. For you who are *not* propeller heads, this means that for each chunk of data, SpiderOak cranks through the encryption process thousands of times more than the original PBKDF2 specification. When dealing with encrypting data, more is better.

Sharing out data is done in one of two ways. The first way is to backup (SpiderOak terminology for upload data) the folder you want to share out. You then create a ShareRoom by selecting the share tab in the SpiderOak application. Next, create a share ID (a public user ID that is used to identify you). Then follow the steps in the wizard to create the ShareRoom. You will have an opportunity to create a specific share password to access the ShareRoom. You can only have folders in the ShareRoom and not individual files. A unique URL is generated once the ShareRoom is created. You can then distribute the URL to anyone you desire.

The second way is to share access to individual files. You accomplish that by navigating to the file from within the SpiderOak application and selecting the link button. SpiderOak then creates a specific URL that will be used to access the file. To protect security, the link is only active for three days.

SpiderOak is also supported on iOS and Android devices. Every time you access SpiderOak from a mobile device or using a web browser you will be required to enter your password. The password (more correctly the encrypted hash of the password) is stored in memory for the duration of the session. It is never written to disk and is removed from memory at the completion of the session. Even though you can access your files from a mobile device, you cannot upload data to your account at this time.

As you can see, SpiderOak is extremely robust in protecting your data via its encryption implementation. This is a highly recommended solution and it is even HIPAA compliant. Give it a try, especially since the entry level package is free.

VIIVO

As promised, we'll describe some products that secure your data before you upload it to one of the cloud-storage providers. Viivo is a product that encrypts your data under your control and works with cloud-storage providers such as Dropbox, OneDrive, Google Drive, and Box. As with most providers, Viivo uses AES-256 to encrypt the files. Like SpiderOak, Viivo uses a variety of encryption methods to deliver the service. There is a free version of Viivo for personal use. Viivo Pro and Viivo for Business are for commercial use, such as your law office. Viivo Pro costs $59.88 per year per user. Viivo for Business includes administrative access and visibility so that you can track users and usage along with many more features. You have to contact Viivo to get pricing for the Viivo for Business product, but there is a free 14-day trial available.

At the base level, Viivo creates a 2048 RSA key pair to exchange encryption keys between devices and users. A Private Key is secured with your password and your password is strengthened using the same Password-Based Key Derivation Function 2 (PBKDF2) Hash Method Authentication Code (HMAC) Secure Hash Authentication 256 (SHA256) that is used with SpiderOak. In other words, it's a fancy way to say that the cryptographic functions utilized provide a high degree of protection.

Viivo stores the security keys separately from Google Drive, OneDrive, Box, or Dropbox. Viivo does not store your keys on their servers, but they do support passphrase recovery through a secure process that uses data on the server along with data on your Viivo-enabled device.

You install the Viivo application on each device where you want to encrypt the data before handing it off to Dropbox, Box, One-Drive, or Google Drive. There are applications available for Mac, Windows, iOS, and Android devices.

Figure 10.2 demonstrates how Viivo works when it has been set up with Dropbox on a PC. Encrypted files are stored in a Dropbox folder called "Viivo-Encrypted." If a user opens this folder and tries to open a file, it won't be accessible. One of three things will happen, depending on the operating system, software, and version. There may be an error message, there may be a message that the file is encrypted, or it may open and look like hieroglyphics. In order to read the file, a user clicks on the desktop icon, like the one at the center of the figure, to open Viivo. Files will be displayed in a window like the one at the bottom of the figure. Clicking on a file here will decrypt it and open it. Saving a file here protects it with encryption. It's easy; that's all there is to it!

Figure 10.2 Using Viivo on a PC

BOXCRYPTOR

Another service that provides for encrypting files before being sent to a cloud-storage provider is Boxcryptor. Boxcryptor is one of the more well-known cloud storage "add-ons." It works with Dropbox, Google Drive, OneDrive, SugarSync, Box, and other major cloud-storage providers. It also supports all cloud-storage services that use the WebDAV standard. That would include providers such as Cubby, Strato HiDrive, and ownCloud.

Boxcryptor creates a virtual drive on your computer, where you place files that need to be encrypted before uploading to your cloud-storage provider. It encrypts individual files using AES-256 and RSA encryption. During the install process, Boxcryptor recommends disabling Windows EFS (Encrypted File System). It is a decent recommendation since EFS is very weak and can be bypassed in a matter of seconds. Therefore, EFS doesn't provide you with any real protection so why not just disable it? You also need to create an account with Boxcryptor and define a password. The password is only known to you and is used to facilitate the encryption. Like many other services, if you lose the password, you will not be able to decrypt any previously encrypted data. This is exactly the feature you want. You want to control the encryption key so that only you can decrypt the data. That's the reason you use a product like Boxcryptor prior to sending data to Dropbox, OneDrive, or any of the other cloud-storage providers.

Boxcryptor has several available versions and is provided on a subscription basis. The Basic version is for individual usage and only includes encrypting the data and sharing files in a secure fashion. It is a free service, but only allows you to connect your virtual Boxcryptor drive to one cloud provider. Only the file contents are encrypted and the filename remains in clear text. The next level of service is called Unlimited Personal and adds additional features. The cost is $48/year for a single user license. In addition to the features of the Basic version, the Unlimited Personal adds encryption of the filenames, synchronization with unlimited cloud providers, unlimited devices, and unlimited support.

There are two commercial use licenses available for your firm. The single user Unlimited Business license costs $96/year and contains all of the features of the Unlimited Personal license. Besides the license authorization to use the product in a commercial setting, you can also assign groups of users to share your files with just a single click. Finally, the Company Package provides enforcement policies, Active Directory support, centralized management, and a single master key to control the encryption. The Company Package is available on a monthly, yearly or three-year basis and for five, ten, 15, 25, or 50 users. The cost is dependent on the number of users and the term. You could spend from $50/month for five users on a monthly basis all the way up to $8,000 for 50 users for three years. Obviously, you can contact Boxcryptor for customized pricing of the Company Package.

Boxcryptor is available for a lot of different computing environments. There are versions available for Windows, Mac, and even Chrome. The mobile versions are for iOS, Android, Windows Phone, Windows RT, and BlackBerry 10.

Boxcryptor is one of the most popular products that we see used in law firms, particularly because it is so flexible and works with a lot of different cloud providers. Remember that you will need to purchase either one of the two business plans for use in your firm. The free Basic license and Unlimited Personal are not to be used in a commercial setting. There are free trials available so make sure you take advantage of them.

NCRYPTEDCLOUD

Another high-end (read expensive) cloud add-on is nCrypted-Cloud. Like other competitors they have a free version for personal use and multiple business solutions. The service works like the others in that the data is encrypted locally with user controlled encryption keys prior to syncing the data to the cloud provider. The commercial options (Small Business, Medium Business, and Enterprise) cost $10 per user per month. The high cost comes from the minimum user requirements for each plan. The Small Business plan requires a minimum of 25 users. The Medium Business plan needs at least 250 users, and the Enterprise level requires 2,500 users. As you can see, the cost is pretty high compared to other services.

However, nCryptedCloud has features that are not available from its competitors. You can set expiration times for file access. Once the timer has expired, the file is no longer shared. In addition, you set a passcode for access to the file. Not only will the user need the link to the shared file, but they'll be required to enter the passcode that you've established. Finally, you can watermark your files. This gives them a type of digital copyright mark discouraging inappropriate usage of the information.

Another cool feature is the amount of logging that nCryptedCloud does. You can view all devices that were used to access data and the users associated with those devices. There's a sort of audit trail too. You can view which policies were set and applied to your data. In addition, you can view all the changes made to the data and when the data was copied or moved.

The cost of this solution will probably scare away most attorneys. However, the features available with nCryptedCloud may sway some firms to accept the cost. This is especially true if you need one of the specific functions mentioned above. Like their competitors, there is a trial available, so give it a spin.

DELL DATA PROTECTION | CLOUD EDITION

Dell Data Protection | Cloud Edition is a part of the Dell Data Protection security suite. It provides powerful enterprise management for the use of cloud services like DropBox, Box, and OneDrive.

It includes control of file access and sharing, auditing, and monitoring, client-side encryption, and central management. It integrates with Dell Data Protection | Mobile Edition to manage use of cloud services on smartphones and tablets. With client-side encryption, the end-users control encryption, not the cloud service provider. It is an enterprise tool and requires a business or law firm server to administer it. For a small or mid-sized firm, the server can be a dedicated PC or part of a PC (virtual server) (http://i.dell.com/sites/doccontent/shared-content/datasheets/en/Documents/Dell_data_protection_cloud_edition__data_sheet_HR.pdf).

ICLOUD

Apple was front and center in the news as nude photographs of celebrities were being posted on the Internet. Leave it to the media to develop the term Celebgate to describe the distribution of the nude selfies. Apple's initial response was that iCloud is secure and the problem was weak user passwords. There was no mention that iCloud allowed unlimited invalid attempts to logon to the account without locking out the user. In fact, Apple was aware of the vulnerability six months prior to the news of Celebgate.[1] Apple quickly updated iCloud to lock out the user after multiple invalid attempts. Prior to the update, you could brute force attack the iCloud password without restriction.

iCloud can synchronize data from your Apple devices and stores the copies on Apple servers. You register each Apple device to iCloud and the data will automatically synchronize between the devices. Apple is similar to many other cloud providers (e.g., Dropbox, Box, etc.) in that they also have the ability to access your data since they hold the encryption key. This means that you need to encrypt any sensitive and confidential data prior to synchronizing with iCloud. In

---

1   The Daily Dot, "Apple knew of iCloud security hole 6 months before Celebgate," http://www.dailydot.com/technology/apple-icloud-brute-force-attack-march/, last modified September 24, 2014.

addition, make sure that you protect your Apple ID and password. Do not share them with anyone as they could be used to steal your identity. All you need is the Apple ID and password to register an Apple device to your iCloud data. The good news is that since Celebgate, Apple has modified the iCloud service so that an e-mail message is sent whenever a new device is registered to iCloud.

OTHER CLOUD SERVICES

Besides cloud storage, the other cloud services that are typically used in a law firm are case management, document assembly, and document management. It is pretty much universal that all the providers encrypt the data in transit using SSL/TLS. That protects the data while it is in motion to and from the provider.

The data at rest may or may not be encrypted. Even if it is encrypted at rest, the vendor can decrypt the data and access the content. In addition, your data is probably stored on media that is shared with other firms and companies. It is not uncommon to have multiple databases for multiple attorneys residing on a single server. The cloud providers do that to maximize usage of their hardware. The problem with this model is that the user does not control the encryption key. Also, there are no products like those mentioned above that encrypt the data before being sent to the cloud provider for using applications like case management. This potentially puts your data at risk since it is accessible to the cloud provider.

Google Apps and Office 365 are two cloud services that are very popular with attorneys, especially solo and small firms. Both offerings are a set of productivity software for functions such as word processing, spreadsheets, presentation slides, etc. Think of it as Microsoft Office, but in the cloud instead of on your computer. When you use Google Apps or Office 365, your data resides on Google's and Microsoft's servers. While the data is encrypted at rest, Google and Microsoft can still access it within the terms of service. This means that you should not store confidential data within Google's or Microsoft's servers. You can still use Google Apps or Office 365 to work on the files, but should store them on devices that you control, unless you use one of the add-on encryption products like BoxCryptor.

Several of the cloud case management providers such as Clio and Rocket Matter contend that encrypting the data at rest would significantly reduce the performance of their applications. They feel that there is enough protection of attorney-client confidential data by the security measures that exist within the application. Perhaps that may be true, but at the end of the day a user's data is accessible to an employee of the cloud provider. We sure would like to have a way to control that encryption and still be able to use cloud-provided applications.

Fortunately, that day may be closer than many think. MIT is working on providing that very function. Raluca Popa, a researcher at MIT, is leading the development of a system called Mylar. The design philosophy is to not trust the server. In our case, that means the cloud application provider. Mylar provides services that keep the data on the servers encrypted at all times and only decrypt it on a user's computer. Your data is encrypted with your own password (we like that control) inside your browser before it goes to the server. The server does not have the ability to decrypt the data.

Mylar also includes some cryptographic tricks so that the server can take action on the data without actually decrypting the contents. As an example, searching across documents that have been uploaded to the server. There are patients at Newton-Wellesley Hospital in Boston that are accessing their medical information on a website that was built using Mylar.

Hopefully, Mylar or some similar technology will ultimately allow the user to control the encryption password and still use all the features of cloud applications in the future. That would go a long way in protecting confidential client information, yet still allow attorneys to use cloud computing for their practices.

Chapter 11
SECURING DOCUMENTS

Protecting individual documents is another area of concern for lawyers. Perhaps you need to store a confidential document in Dropbox and haven't obtained one of the pre-encryption services discussed in the cloud chapter. You can secure documents and other files very easily. Merely locking the file with a password encrypts the contents in current versions of Microsoft Office, Adobe Acrobat, and WinZip. Just like other authentication methods, you need to make sure you are using a complex password or passphrase to secure the document. The password should be long (14 characters or more), contain lower and upper case letters, contain numbers, and perhaps some symbols too. Having a weak password makes it fairly easy to achieve a brute force crack.

Figure 11.1

These days, any advanced intruder with the right equipment can crack any eight-character password in about six hours.[1] Sad to say, most experts now recommend a 14-character password—alphanumeric with special characters.

---

1   "8-character passwords just got a lot easier to crack." *NBC News.* http://www.nbcnews.com/tech/security/8-character-passwords-just-got-lot-easier-crack-f1C7530242. Accessed October 14, 2014.

So what files are typically password protected? Putting an open password on any Microsoft Office file (e.g. Word document, Excel spreadsheet, PowerPoint presentation, etc.) encrypts the contents. Office 2010 files are encrypted using AES-128–bit encryption and Office 2013 files are encrypted using AES-256–bit encryption. Perhaps the increased encryption strength is a good reason to upgrade to Office 2013 if you haven't done so already. Besides Office files, setting an open password for an Adobe Acrobat file encrypts the file too. You can encrypt files within a WinZip archive too, which we'll cover in this chapter.

MICROSOFT OFFICE

As previously mentioned, you can secure confidential data in a Microsoft Office file by placing a password on the file. The process is similar for Word, Excel, PowerPoint, etc. so we'll just use Word as an example. Office 2010 encrypts using AES-128–bit encryption and Office 2013 uses AES-256–bit encryption. The process is the same for both products.

Once you are ready to protect your Word document, select the **File** tab and then click the **Protect Document** button in the **Permissions** section. Next select the Encrypt with Password option as

Figure 11.2

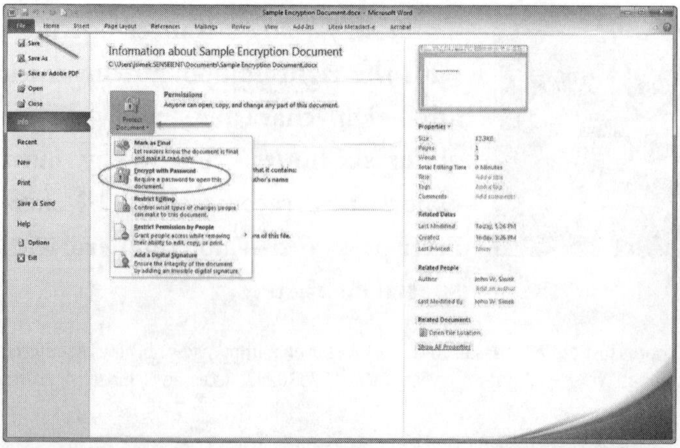

shown in Figure 11.2. You will then be presented with a dialog box to enter a password as shown in Figure 11.3.

Figure 11.3

Enter a password to encrypt the document. Remember to use a strong password (length and complexity) to maximize the protection of the data. Once you have protected the document, it is now safe to send along as an attachment. You will need to share the password with the recipient of the file so that he or she can open it, but don't send it along in clear text along with the attachment. Call the recipient or send a separate e-mail (hopefully encrypted!) at a later time.

That's all there is to encrypting a Microsoft Office file. Simple, painless and secure, as long as you use a strong password.

ADOBE ACROBAT

With Microsoft Office files the encryption method is determined by the version of Office that is used (AES-128–bit or AES-256–bit). With Adobe Acrobat, you can determine the encryption method, which is based on the amount of backward compatibility with other Acrobat versions you desire. So let's get started.

Open the PDF that you want to encrypt. Select **File** and then **Properties** . . . from the menu choice. This will bring up the **Document Properties** dialog box (Figure 11.4).

Figure 11.4

Select the **Password Security** option from the dropdown menu. Click the **OK** button. You will then be presented with the **Password Security—Settings** dialog box as shown in Figure 11.5.

Figure 11.5

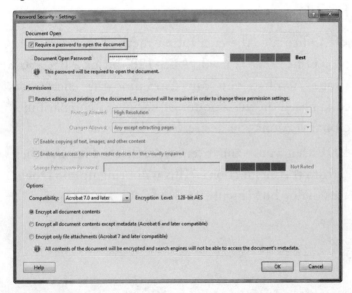

In the **Document Open** section, check the box to **Require a password to open the document**. Enter your password into the **Document Open Password** field. You will notice that Adobe attempts to "score" your password. The goal is to get all four green bars with a **Best** rating. Leave the **Encrypt all document contents** radio button selected in the **Options** section. Finally, select the appropriate encryption level. This is done by changing the pull down selection in the **Compatibility** option. You have the following choices as to compatibility and encryption:

1. Acrobat 6.0 and later—Encryption Level: 128-bit RC4
2. Acrobat 7.0 and later—Encryption Level: 128-bit AES
3. Acrobat X and later—Encryption Level: 256-bit AES

As you can see, the stronger the encryption level, the less backward compatibility with older Acrobat versions. Since many attorneys may not be running the later versions of Acrobat, the default setting of Acrobat 7 and later is probably sufficient encryption strength. At least it's AES encryption and not the much weaker RC4. When all of your selections are complete, click on the **OK** button. You will be prompted to verify the **Document Open Password**. Type in the password again and click the **OK** button. A warning dialog box will appear (assuming you have not previously checked the **Do not show this message again**) reminding you that the security settings will not be applied until you save the file.

Figure 11.6

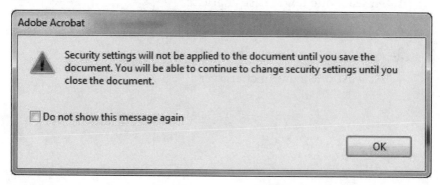

Once you save the file, the contents are encrypted. You can then safely send the protected PDF as an attachment to an e-mail message. Just like the Word example above, you will need to tell the recipient what the password is, but not in the same message as the attachment.

WINZIP

Another option for securing data with encryption is to use WinZip. WinZip has two methods of encryption available to the user, which we'll cover shortly. Just like Microsoft Office files and Adobe Acrobat, WinZip encryption is controlled through passwords. WinZip can be configured to establish the minimum requirements for encryption passwords. First, go to the **Settings** tab and select the **WinZip Options** icon as shown in Figure 11.7.

Figure 11.7

The **WinZip Options** dialog box will launch. Select the **Passwords** tab. This is where you configure the minimum password requirements. Select the minimum character length for passwords. There are four password characteristics available for selection.

1. At least one lower case character

2. At least one upper case character

3. At least one numeric character

4. At least one symbol character

Figure 11.8

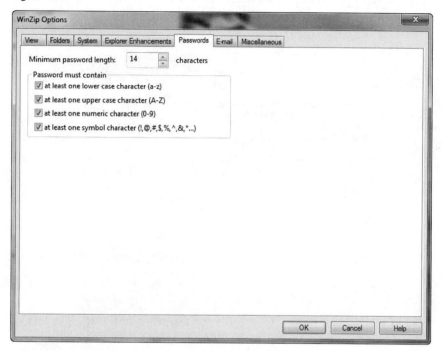

When you have completed your selections, click on the **OK** button. You then set the default method of encryption that WinZip will use. From the **Setting** tab, select the **Conversion Settings** icon and then **Encryption** as shown in Figure 11.9.

Figure 11.9

The **Encryption Options** dialog box will launch, where you select the desired encryption method.

Figure 11.10

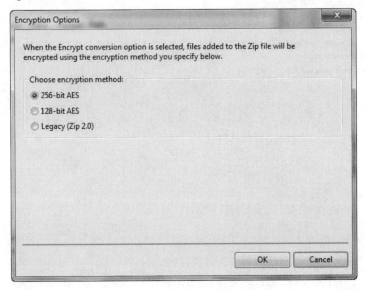

There are two types of AES encryption provided by WinZip, as can be seen in Figure 11.10. The Zip 2.0 encryption is much weaker and should only be used when distributing Zip files to recipients with much older versions of WinZip. Zip 2.0 encryption only protects against the casual user and not those who have access to password recovery tools. The AES encryption is much stronger and should be used as the default. AES-encrypted files are supported in WinZip 9.0 and later versions.

Next we'll cover the steps to encrypt the contents of the WinZip file. The most efficient way to encrypt files is while they are being added to a WinZip archive. To encrypt the files as they are being added, check the **Encrypt added files** selection in the **Options** section and click the **Add** button as shown in Figure 11.11. You will be presented with a warning concerning the advantages and disadvantages of the various encryption methods. Click the **OK** button to proceed or select the **Help** button for more information.

Figure 11.11

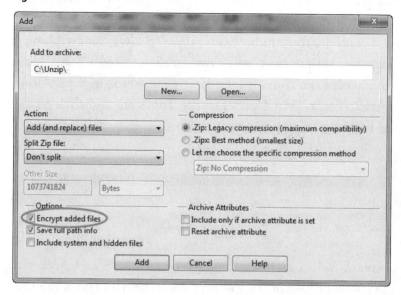

Enter the password and re-enter the password for confirmation (Figure 11.12). Notice that the password policy requirements are listed to remind you of the password characteristics.

Figure 11.12

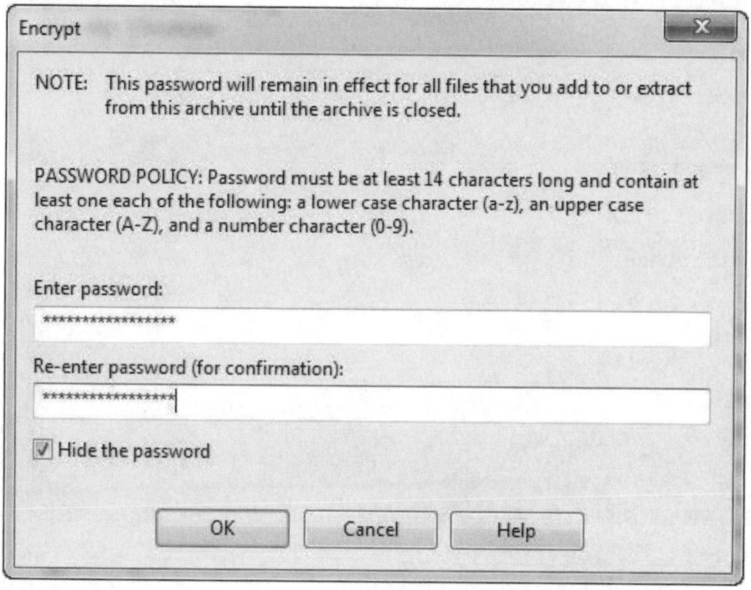

A dialog box with compression statistics is displayed next. Click the OK button and you have successfully created a Zip file with encrypted content. You can now send the Zip file as an attachment to the intended recipients. If you have already created a Zip file and decide to encrypt the contents at a later time, here's how you do it. Open the Zip file in WinZip. Select the **Tools** tab and click on the **Selected Files** icon in the **Convert** section.

Figure 11.13

A **Convert Selected Files** dialog box will launch. Check the option to **Encrypt files** in the **Encryption** section and click the **OK** button (Figure 11.14). Enter the encryption password and continue with the other steps previously described.

Figure 11.14

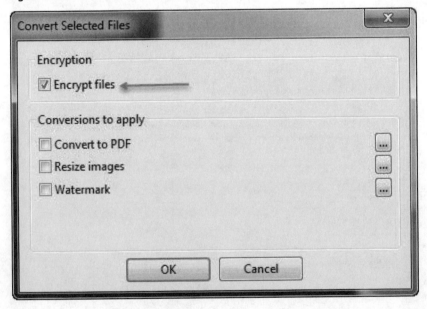

Even though WinZip uses AES encryption, attorneys should be aware of the limitations. The encryption only applies to the contents of the files in the Zip archive. Information about the files themselves, such as name, date, size, attributes, CRC, and compression ratio are all stored in unencrypted form. This means that anybody can view the file information (not the contents) without a password. WinZip encryption is not the same thing as authentication. The password is not needed for actions that do not involve the decryption of the file contents. Specifically, encrypted files can be deleted from a Zip file or can be renamed within the Zip file. Also, you can add unencrypted files to the Zip archive without knowing the encryption password for the other files. As with any encryption method, password strength has a big impact. Make sure you use strong passwords when encrypting data.

STEGANOGRAPHY

While not technically an encryption method, steganography can be used to protect data. Some people call steganography an art, some call it a science, and some call it an art and a science. No matter what label you put on it, steganography is the concealing of data within other data. In other words, hiding a message within an image file. It works by replacing bits of useless or unused data in normal electronic files. Steganography is commonly used when encryption is not permitted or to supplement encryption. Special software is needed for steganography, some of which is freely available on the Internet.

In the majority of cases, you will not be able to determine if steganography is even being used. Besides special software to "inject" the hidden data into a normal file, detection software is also needed to determine the existence of steganography. While we don't expect most attorneys will be using steganography or encounter it on a daily basis, it is another potential way to protect confidential information. If nothing else, it may be something to play around with on a quiet weekend.

If you look up steganography on Wikipedia, you'll find a photo of trees which "hides" a photo of a cat. Interesting and innocent, but the fear has been that terrorists will use "steg," as it is called for short, to communicate the details of plots.

We have yet to see a lawyer using steganography, but at least now you know what it is!

Chapter 12
THE FUTURE OF ENCRYPTION: THROUGH A GLASS, DARKLY

Do you remember the memorable scene from the 1967 movie *The Graduate* where the conversation went like this?

Mr. McGuire: "I just want to say one word to you. Just one word."

Benjamin: "Yes, sir."

Mr. McGuire: "Are you listening?"

Benjamin: "Yes, I am."

Mr. McGuire: "Plastics."

Well, if we're going to discuss the future of encryption, we want to say just two words to you.

Just two words.

Are you listening?

QUANTUM PHYSICS

When brilliant scientists talk about the future of encryption, quantum physics dominates the conversation.

The father of quantum physics is Max Planck, pictured at left in 1930. He originated quantum theory and was awarded the Nobel Prize in Physics in 1918. Even as a young man (right), he always seemed to look serious!

Figure 12.1   **Figure 12.2**

Want to know what kind of thoughts made him look so serious?

Look at this Wikipedia definition of quantum mechanics, also known as quantum physics or quantum theory:

> Quantum mechanics is a fundamental branch of physics which deals with physical phenomena at nanoscopic scales where the action is on the order of the Planck constant. It departs from classical mechanics primarily at the quantum realm of atomic and subatomic length scales. Quantum mechanics provides a mathematical description of much of the dual particle-like and wave-like behavior and interactions of energy and matter. Quantum mechanics provides a substantially useful framework for many features of the modern periodic table of elements including the behavior of atoms during chemical bonding and has played a significant role in the development of many modern technologies.

Your head is no doubt spinning just reading the words.

But don't worry, the late Nobel laureate Richard Feynman, regarded as one of the pioneers of quantum computing, was fond of saying, "If you think you understand quantum mechanics, you don't understand quantum mechanics."[1]

Can it be simplified? Yes, but recognize that any explanation that is somewhat simple has been watered down considerably. But here goes. The computers we use today must do one calculation at a time. A quantum computer can avoid making unnecessary calculations to solve a problem. So it gets the right answer much faster.

QUANTUM COMPUTING

Quantum computing is based on the "quantum superposition"—the belief that an object simultaneously exists in all states. Our computers use binary bits, which are either ones or zeroes. A quantum computer uses quantum bits—generally called qubits by the scientists—which are simultaneously zero and one. We know—it is mind-bending to think about.

Quantum computers are incredibly fragile. They can be built with individual atoms, photons, or electrons. They must be completely isolated from external environments. If they are not, they may become unstable and their calculations rendered useless. They are therefore housed in room-size metal Farraday boxes, which are secured against any electromagnetic leaks.

And they don't, yet, work over great distances. More than 60 miles (there is some dispute over the effective distance) and the

---

1   "NSA seeks to build quantum computer that could crack most types of encryption," *Washington Post*, January 2, 2014. http://www.washingtonpost.com/world/national-security/nsa-seeks-to-build-quantum-computer-that-could-crack-most-types-of-encryption/2014/01/02/8fff297e-7195-11e3-8def-a33011492df2_story.html. Accessed October 10, 2014.

photon signals fade. And they are not very scalable. The true believers will give you rosy projections of the present and future of quantum computing. We have even seen them say that "it is ultra-secure—it is a future-proof technology."[2]

As if there were any such thing.

We prefer the cautionary words of the National Institute of Standards Technology (NIST), which doesn't believe quantum computing is yet viable for production systems. Alan Mink, an electronics engineer in NIST's Advanced Networking Division, has said "It's a complicated protocol and the limitations of implementing the technology have not yet been overcome."[3]

Who is trying to build them? Practically everyone—just look at the potential to unlock the secrets of all corporations, banks, and governments. We know from the Edward Snowden leaks that the NSA is in the race to build "a cryptologically useful quantum computer" with a $70.7 million research program called "Penetrating Hard Targets."[4] Much of the work is hosted through classified contracts at a lab in College Park, Maryland, and funded by "black money."

This brought to mind the quote from character Julius Levinson in the move *Independence Day*: "You don't actually think they spend $20,000 on a hammer, $30,000 on a toilet seat, do you?" So don't go looking for these monies in the federal budget.

If the NSA or any of the other runners in this race are successful, that would mean that current forms of public key encryption would be broken. And all historical secrets, many of which have long-term value, would be broken. A number of experts think that the NSA is roughly in the same place as the European Union and Switzerland

---

2 "Future-Proof Encryption," *Communications of the ACM*. http://cacm.acm.org/magazines/2013/11/169023-future-proof-encryption/fulltext. Accessed October 10, 2014.

3 "Can Quantum Cryptography Work in the Real World?" *GCN*. http://gcn.com/articles/2013/10/28/quantum-cryptography.aspx. Accessed October 10, 2014.

4 *Id.*

in its research, with no immediate breakthroughs in sight but a lot of solid research in place.

RSA encryption, on which we've relied for so long, would simply be obsolete in an era where quantum computers rule. RSA is used because it is so hard to factor the product of two large prime numbers. You can't break the encryption without finding those two numbers and it takes **forever** on conventional computers.

Back in 2009, scientists were able to discover the primes within a 768-bit number but it took hundreds of computers and nearly two years to do it. The same scientists predicted that it would take 1,000 times longer to break a 1,024-bit encryption key, which is used often today. For a quantum computer, this would be a simple task. Some companies are moving to using 2,048-bit keys, but even those are thought to be crackable by quantum computers. The point is that, if you can try every possible combination (brute force), eventually you will discover the answer. Quantum computing makes the brute force crack (trying every possible combination of letters, numbers, and special characters) a very realistic probability.

So when are we going to see these marvels? "Expert" guesses, which sound much like SWAGs to us, range from five to 100 years. Small quantum computers already exist, but "small" won't revolutionize decryption.

Because quantum computers are so very fragile, building them with enough qubits is a challenge. Even the NSA is only talking about having "dynamical decoupling and complete quantum control on two semiconductor qubits."[5]

Two, just two. A quantum computer that could break strong encryption would need hundreds or thousands of qubits. But suppose, which is starting to seem realistic, that it takes another five to ten years to achieve breakthrough in quantum computing. When do you need to start worrying?

---

5 *Id.*

The correct answer, according to all the experts, is **now**.

Fighting back to protect privacy against the formidable capabilities of quantum computers is a nightmare of unimaginable proportions. We haven't yet seen anyone of repute suggest that there is a way to "outrun" quantum computers.

That makes these days seem innocent indeed. In our immediate future, we are seeing end-to-end encryption adopted by giants like Yahoo, Facebook, and Google—and others are following in line at a breakneck pace. This is not new—it has been available for some time through tools such as Pretty Good Privacy and Gnu Privacy Guard (GnuPG), but it never went mainstream—until now.

End-to-end encryption is a lot simpler than quantum computing—it simply means that data is encrypted as it travels from your computer to a recipient's computer. There is no way for the government—or anyone else—to go to a secret FISA court to get the service provider to cough up the data. The service providers won't have it. The government (at least today) would have to go to the individual.

Edward Snowden, in a 2014 interview, said, "The result is a more constitutional, more carefully overseen enforcement model. If they want to gather each user's communications, they have to go to them specifically."[6] And that, of course, would mean the word would get out—no more of NSA and others operating secretly in the dark with the providers forced to comply with gag orders.

Long term though, it is quantum computing that will rule us. And what happens when the quantum computers break our encryption schemes?

The best guess seems to be that we will learn to use quantum computers against other quantum computers. We know your head is throbbing by now, but imagine a world in which quantum encryption generates its own keys (through photons) but not in the same

---

6   "A Call for a Highly Encrypted Future," *New York Times*. http://bits.blogs.nytimes.com/2014/03/12/a-call-for-a-highly-encrypted-future/?_php=true&_type=blogs&_r=0. Accessed October 10, 2014.

way as PGP and others. If someone attempted to intercept a quantum-encrypted communication, it would create an anomaly that would warn the encryption system, which would abort the communication and alert the user. Far-fetched? Not really—scientists are working it out as we write.[7]

One good description of quantum cryptography was penned by Gregory Mone for the Association for Computing Machinery. Using the redoubtable "Alice and Bob" of what he calls "the crypto world" he describes the process pretty clearly:

> If two people, dubbed Alice and Bob in the crypto world, want to communicate securely, they first generate and exchange a shared, secret key. This key, which is as long as the message itself, as opposed to the relatively short 128-bit or 256-bit keys used in today's systems, is known as a one-time pad, and is only used once. Alice encrypts her message with the one-time pad, then sends it to Bob, who applies the same key to unscramble the text.
>
> The quantum aspect of the process lies in how they generate and exchange that key. In the most common method, known as prepare and measure, Alice sends photons of light to Bob. A photon can assume a number of possible states—different spins and polarizations—that can be used to represent different bits. So, a photon with a vertical orientation might stand in for the bit 1, while a photon that is horizontally oriented could correspond to 0. Alice prepares each photon, collapsing it into a particular state, then sends it to Bob, who attempts to measure the result. They each translate what they see into key bits and compare their results.
>
> If someone tries to spy on the process and intercept the photons en route, then Alice and Bob will notice too many discrepancies and conclude the line of communication is insecure. But if the measurements match often enough, they are left with a matching string of random bits they can use as a shared, secret key to encrypt and then decipher a message.

---

7   "Quantum Encryption Could Be Coming Soon to Mobile Payments," *Motherboard.* http://mother board.vice.com/read/quantum-encryption-could-be-coming-soon-to-mobile-payments. Accessed October 10, 2014.

The security of the key stems from the fact it relies on photons, not factoring. "The laws of physics say that if I am sending light, any attempt by an eavesdropper to make a measurement on that must create a disturbance," says quantum communications expert Jeffrey Shapiro of the Massachusetts Institute of Technology. "What Alice and Bob rely on to get their security is that law of physics. That is a different trust model than saying we know this is a computationally difficult problem and therefore we can rely on the fact that no one has a computer powerful enough to break this system.[8]

Quantum physics may also make possible the building of a "one-shot" memory unit, whose contents can only be read once. Using a technique called "conjugate coding," two secret messages, such as authorization codes, can be encoded into the same string of qubits, allowing a user to retrieve either one of the two messages, but not both. And the messages can only be read once.

The risk in this approach comes from a quantum phenomenon called "entanglement," where two particles can impact one another even when they are separated by great distances. If an adversary were to use entanglement effectively, he could retrieve both messages at once, breaking the security. As computer scientist Yi-Kai Liu has said, "It's fascinating how entanglement—and the lack thereof—is the key to making this work."[9]

And you thought entanglement was something that happened to Christmas tree lights. It's a whole new world.

If you find yourself, at the end of this book, feeling entirely entangled with no hope of becoming disentangled, you may be forgiven. There is nothing easy about understanding quantum computing and those closest to the subject argue over the fine points—even the not-so-fine points—vociferously and at length.

---

8   "Future-Proof Encryption," *Communications of the ACM* on/fulltext" http://cacm.acm.org/magazines/2013/11/169023-future-proof-encryption/fulltext. Accessed October 10, 2014.

9   http://www.nist.gov/itl/math/onetime-011414.cfm.

But whatever the final truths of the future of encryption, there is no doubt that, for our foreseeable future, you don't need goat entrails or tea leaves to know that quantum computing is on its way and that it will forever disrupt the cryptography world. Lawyers, in order to protect their confidential data, are going to need to keep an eye on quantum computing developments.

But for now, breathe a sigh of relief and simply rely on the words of cybersecurity guru Bruce Schneier: "Strong cryptography drives the NSA batty."[10]

So encrypt away and you are likely safe—for now.

---

10 https://www.schneier.com/news/archives/2014/02/schneier_nsa_snoopin.html.

An Encryption Quick Start Action Plan

An American Bar Association resolution adopted in August 2014 "encourages private and public sector organizations to develop, implement, and maintain an appropriate cybersecurity program that complies with applicable ethical and legal obligations, and is tailored to the nature and scope of the organization, and the data and systems to be protected." It covers attorneys and law firms, as well as other businesses and enterprises. An appropriate information security or cybersecurity program is an essential part of compliance with attorneys' duty under ABA Model Rule 1.6(c) to employ "reasonable efforts to prevent the inadvertent or unauthorized disclosure of, or unauthorized access to, information relating to the representation of a client." Encryption of data is a critical component of an appropriate information security or cybersecurity program (Chapters 2 and 3).

This Quick Start Action Plan outlines the steps that attorneys can take to implement encryption—**starting now.**

1. Start with the basics for encryption that you are using now or implementing in the future (Chapters 4–7).

   a. If you need help in implementing encryption, find someone who is qualified to assist you.

   b. Protect encrypted data with strong authentication. In many implementations of encryption, access to the decryption key is protected by the user's password or passphrase. Make sure that you have strong passwords or passphrases for encryption you are currently using or you plan to implement in the future.

   c. Back up data. Like other areas of technology, there can be technical failures with encryption hardware and software. Keep a secure backup of encrypted data, a step that should always be done, even for data that is not encrypted.

   d. Back up the recovery keys. In some implementations of encryption, a user can back up a recovery key that *may* make encrypted data recoverable if a user forgets a password or there is a technology problem. Back up the recovery key in a secure place. In mid-sized and larger firms, recovery keys should be managed by IT staff.

2. Start **with the "no-brainer" encryption solutions—encryption of laptops, smartphones, tablets, and portable drives** (Chapters 5, 6, and 7). The Verizon 2014 *Data Breach Investigation Report* notes that "encryption is as close to a no-brainer solution as it gets" to protect confidential data on lost or stolen laptops and mobile devices. It's not just Verizon, this view is widely held by information security professionals and government agencies. Review the devices that you and your firm are using—laptops, smartphones, tablets, and portable drives—and make plans to encrypt them as soon as reasonably possible if they are not already encrypted. With many of them, it's just

a matter of turning encryption on. Consider encryption and enable it when you add new devices.

3. Protect **confidential documents with encryption**—*a solution you already have* (Chapter 11). Confidential documents transmitted electronically or by e-mail should be protected by encryption. Current versions of Microsoft Office, Adobe Acrobat, and WinZip encrypt documents when password protection is used. New Jersey Ethics Opinion 701 (April 2006—more than eight years ago) advised attorneys to password-protect documents [encrypt them] when they are sent over the Internet (Chapter 2). While this form of encryption may not be as secure as some of the other solutions discussed in the book, it is much more secure than no encryption and is immediately available to most attorneys.

4. Use **secure network connections** (Chapter 8). Confidential data that is transmitted outside of a secure network should be protected. This requires secure connections between networks and over the Internet. Review the various network connections that you and your firm use and make sure that they are secure. For the Internet, you should use https:// or virtual private networks as a minimum.

5. Secure **your wireless networks** (Chapter 8). Make sure that your law office wireless network and home networks used for client data are protected by WPA2 (Wi-Fi Protected Access 2) encryption and are securely configured. If you are using an older wireless access device that does not support WPA2, replace it.

6. Be **careful on public networks** (Chapter 8). Make sure that you can use a public network securely for confidential data **before** you use it, or avoid using it. Use only secure connections—https:// or a virtual private network.

7. Implement **an encrypted e-mail solution** (Chapter 9). It has now reached the point where most or all attorneys should have the ability to use encrypted e-mail, where appropriate, for confidential communications. A basic level of protection can be provided by putting the confidential communication in a password-protected/encrypted attachment. There are now a number of easy to use, inexpensive options that are available for securing e-mail, including ones for solos and small firms.

8. Use **encryption in the cloud** (Chapter 10). Encryption controlled by the end-user should be the default for confidential data stored in the cloud. End-user–controlled encryption should be required for attorneys unless the attorney makes an informed decision that the data is not sensitive enough to require this level of protection or that the cloud-service provider will implement and maintain sufficient security controls without end-user controlled encryption. For attorneys, this requires the analysis required by the ethics rules and opinions discussed in Chapter 2, including competent and reasonable measures to safeguard information relating to clients, due diligence concerning service providers, and requiring service providers to safeguard data in accordance with attorneys' confidentiality obligations.

Glossary

Please note that the following Glossary of Key Information Security Terms from the National Institute of Standards and Technology (NIST) contains only selected information security terms and definitions. The full May 2013 version of the Glossary may be found at http://nvlpubs.nist.gov/nistpubs/ir/2013/NIST.IR.7298r2.pdf. This is not easy reading—we have tried to explain many of the terms in plain English (as much as possible) in this book, but it would be a disservice not to give you the NIST definitions, which govern the cybersecurity world.

Access Point	A device that logically connects wireless client devices operating in infrastructure to one another and provides access to a distribution system, if connected, which is typically an organization's enterprise wired network. SOURCE: SP 800-48; SP 800-121
Ad Hoc Network	A wireless network that dynamically connects wireless client devices to each other without the use of an infrastructure device, such as an access point or a base station. SOURCE: SP 800-121

Advanced Encryption Standard—(AES)

The Advanced Encryption Standard specifies a U.S. government-approved cryptographic algorithm that can be used to protect electronic data. The AES algorithm is a symmetric block cipher that can encrypt (encipher) and decrypt (decipher) information. This standard specifies the Rijndael algorithm, a symmetric block cipher that can process data blocks of 128 bits, using cipher keys with lengths of 128, 192, and 256 bits.

SOURCE: FIPS 197

A U.S. government-approved cryptographic algorithm that can be used to protect electronic data. The AES algorithm is a symmetric block cipher that can encrypt (encipher) and decrypt (decipher) information.

SOURCE: CNSSI-4009

Assurance

Grounds for confidence that the other four security goals (integrity, availability, confidentiality, and accountability) have been adequately met by a specific implementation. "Adequately met" includes (1) functionality that performs correctly, (2) sufficient protection against unintentional errors (by users or software), and (3) sufficient resistance to intentional penetration or by-pass.

SOURCE: SP 800-27

The grounds for confidence that the set of intended security controls in an information system are effective in their application.

SOURCE: SP 800-37; SP 800-53A

Measure of confidence that the security features, practices, procedures, and architecture of an information system accurately mediate and enforce the security policy.

SOURCE: CNSSI-4009; SP 800-39

Asymmetric Cryptography	See Public Key Cryptography.
Asymmetric Keys	Two related keys, a public key and a private key, that are used to perform complementary operations, such as encryption and decryption or signature generation and signature verification.
	SOURCE: FIPS 201
Bit	A contraction of the term Binary Digit. The smallest unit of information in a binary system of notation.
	SOURCE: CNSSI-4009
	A binary digit having a value of 0 or 1.
	SOURCE: FIPS 180-4
Bit Error Rate	Ratio between the number of bits incorrectly received and the total number of bits transmitted in a telecommunications system.
	SOURCE: CNSSI-4009
Block	Sequence of binary bits that comprise the input, output, State, and Round Key. The length of a sequence is the number of bits it contains. Blocks are also interpreted as arrays of bytes.
	SOURCE: FIPS 197
Block Cipher	A symmetric key cryptographic algorithm that transforms a block of information at a time using a cryptographic key. For a block cipher algorithm, the length of the input block is the same as the length of the output block.
	SOURCE: SP 800-90
Block Cipher Algorithm	A family of functions and their inverses that is parameterized by a cryptographic key; the function maps bit strings of a fixed length to bit strings of the same length.
	SOURCE: SP 800-67

Bulk Encryption	Simultaneous encryption of all channels of a multichannel telecommunications link. SOURCE: CNSSI-4009
Certificate	A digital representation of information that at least: 1) identifies the certification authority issuing it, 2) names or identifies its subscriber, 3) contains the subscriber's public key, 4) identifies its operational period, and 5) is digitally signed by the certification authority issuing it. SOURCE: SP 800-32
Certificate Management	Process whereby certificates (as defined above) are generated, stored, protected, transferred, loaded, used, and destroyed. SOURCE: CNSSI-4009
Certificate Management Authority—(CMA)	A Certification Authority (CA) or a Registration Authority (RA). SOURCE: SP 800-32
Certificate Policy (CP)	A specialized form of administrative policy tuned to electronic transactions performed during certificate management. A Certificate Policy addresses all aspects associated with the generation, production, distribution, accounting, compromise recovery, and administration of digital certificates. Indirectly, a Certificate Policy can also govern the transactions conducted using a communications system protected by a certificate-based security system. By controlling critical certificate extensions, such policies and associated enforcement technology can support provision of the security services required by particular applications. SOURCE: CNSSI-4009; SP 800-32

Certificate Status Authority	A trusted entity that provides online verification to a Relying Party of a subject certificate's trustworthiness, and may also provide additional attribute information for the subject certificate. SOURCE: SP 800-32; CNSSI-4009
Certification Authority (CA)	A trusted entity that issues and revokes public key certificates. SOURCE: FIPS 201 The entity in a public key infrastructure (PKI) that is responsible for issuing certificates and exacting compliance to a PKI policy. SOURCE: SP 800-21; FIPS 186 1. For Certification and Accreditation (C&A) (C&A Assessment): Official responsible for performing the comprehensive evaluation of the security features of an information system and determining the degree to which it meets its security requirements 2. For Public Key Infrastructure (PKI): A trusted third party that issues digital certificates and verifies the identity of the holder of the digital certificate. SOURCE: CNSSI-4009
Cipher	Series of transformations that converts plaintext to ciphertext using the Cipher Key. SOURCE: FIPS 197
Cipher Block Chaining-Message Authentication Code (CBC-MAC)	A secret-key block-cipher algorithm used to encrypt data and to generate a Message Authentication Code (MAC) to provide assurance that the payload and the associated data are authentic. SOURCE: SP 800-38C

Cipher Suite	Negotiated algorithm identifiers. Cipher suites are identified in human-readable form using a pneumonic code.
	SOURCE: SP 800-52
CipherText Auto-Key (CTAK)	Cryptographic logic that uses previous ciphertext to generate a key stream.
	SOURCE: CNSSI-4009
Ciphertext/Cipher Text	Data output from the Cipher or input to the Inverse Cipher.
	SOURCE: FIPS 197
	Data in its enciphered form.
	SOURCE: SP 800-56B
Clear Text	Information that is not encrypted.
	SOURCE: SP 800-82
Cloud Computing	A model for enabling on-demand network access to a shared pool of configurable IT capabilities/resources (e.g., networks, servers, storage, applications, and services) that can be rapidly provisioned and released with minimal management effort or service provider interaction. It allows users to access technology-based services from the network cloud without knowledge of, expertise with, or control over the technology infrastructure that supports them. This cloud model is composed of five essential characteristics (on-demand self-service, ubiquitous network access, location independent resource pooling, rapid elasticity, and measured service); three service delivery models (Cloud Software as a Service [SaaS], Cloud Platform as a Service [PaaS], and Cloud Infrastructure as a Service [IaaS]); and four models for enterprise access (Private cloud, Community cloud, Public cloud, and Hybrid cloud).

Note: Both the user's data and essential security services may reside in and be managed within the network cloud.

Source: CNSSI-4009

Computer Cryptography
Use of a crypto-algorithm program by a computer to authenticate or encrypt/decrypt information.

Source: CNSSI-4009

Controlled Cryptographic Item (CCI) Assembly
Device embodying a cryptographic logic or other COMSEC design that NSA has approved as a Controlled Cryptographic Item (CCI). It performs the entire COMSEC function, but depends upon the host equipment to operate.

Source: CNSSI-4009

Controlled Cryptographic Item (CCI) Component
Part of a Controlled Cryptographic Item (CCI) that does not perform the entire COMSEC function but depends upon the host equipment, or assembly, to complete and operate the COMSEC function.

Source: CNSSI-4009

Counter with Cipher Block Chaining-Message Authentication Code (CCM)
A mode of operation for a symmetric key block cipher algorithm. It combines the techniques of the Counter (CTR) mode and the Cipher Block Chaining-Message Authentication Code (CBC-MAC) algorithm to provide assurance of the confidentiality and the authenticity of computer data.

Source: SP 800-38C

Cross-Certificate
A certificate used to establish a trust relationship between two Certification Authorities.

Source: SP 800-32; CNSSI-4009

Cross-Domain Capabilities
The set of functions that enable the transfer of information between security domains in

accordance with the policies of the security domains involved.

SOURCE: CNSSI-4009

Cross-Domain Solution (CDS)

A form of controlled interface that provides the ability to manually and/or automatically access and/or transfer information between different security domains.

SOURCE: CNSSI-4009; SP 800-37

Cryptanalysis

1) Operations performed in defeating cryptographic protection without an initial knowledge of the key employed in providing the protection.

2) The study of mathematical techniques for attempting to defeat cryptographic techniques and information system security. This includes the process of looking for errors or weaknesses in the implementation of an algorithm or of the algorithm itself.

SOURCE: SP 800-57 Part 1; CNSSI-4009

Cryptographic Alarm

Circuit or device that detects failures or aberrations in the logic or operation of crypto-equipment. Crypto-alarm may inhibit transmission or may provide a visible and/or audible alarm.

SOURCE: CNSSI-4009

Cryptographic Algorithm

A well-defined computational procedure that takes variable inputs, including a cryptographic key, and produces an output.

SOURCE: SP 800-21; CNSSI-4009

Cryptographic Hash Function

A function that maps a bit string of arbitrary length to a fixed-length bit string. Approved hash functions satisfy the following properties:

1) (One-way) It is computationally infeasible to find any input that maps to any pre-specified output, and

2) (Collision resistant) It is computationally infeasible to find any two distinct inputs that map to the same output.

SOURCE: SP 800-21

Cryptographic Ignition Key (CIK)

Device or electronic key used to unlock the secure mode of crypto-equipment.

SOURCE: CNSSI-4009

Cryptographic Initialization

Function used to set the state of a cryptographic logic prior to key generation, encryption, or other operating mode.

SOURCE: CNSSI-4009

Cryptographic Key

A value used to control cryptographic operations, such as decryption, encryption, signature generation, or signature verification.

SOURCE: SP 800-63

Cryptographic Logic

The embodiment of one (or more) cryptographic algorithm(s), along with alarms, checks, and other processes essential to effective and secure performance of the cryptographic process(es).

SOURCE: CNSSI-4009

Cryptographic Material—(slang CRYPTO)

COMSEC material used to secure or authenticate information.

SOURCE: CNSSI-4009

Cryptographic Module

The set of hardware, software, firmware, or some combination thereof that implements cryptographic logic or processes, including cryptographic algorithms, and is contained within the cryptographic boundary of the module.

SOURCE: SP 800-32; FIPS 196

Cryptographic Module Security Policy	A precise specification of the security rules under which a cryptographic module will operate, including the rules derived from the requirements of this standard (FIPS 140-2) and additional rules imposed by the vendor.
	SOURCE: FIPS 140-2
Cryptographic Module Validation Program (CMVP)	Validates cryptographic modules to Federal Information Processing Standard (FIPS) 140-2 and other cryptography-based standards. The CMVP is a joint effort between National Institute of Standards and Technology (NIST) and the Communications Security Establishment (CSE) of the government of Canada. Products validated as conforming to FIPS 140-2 are accepted by the federal agencies of both countries for the protection of sensitive information (United States) or designated information (Canada). The goal of the CMVP is to promote the use of validated cryptographic modules and provide federal agencies with a security metric to use in procuring equipment containing validated cryptographic modules.
	SOURCE: FIPS 140-2
Cryptographic Net	Stations holding a common key.
	SOURCE: CNSSI-4009
Cryptographic Period	Time span during which each key setting remains in effect.
	SOURCE: CNSSI-4009
Cryptographic Product	A cryptographic key (public, private, or shared) or public key certificate, used for encryption, decryption, digital signature, or signature verification; and other items, such as compromised key lists (CKL) and certificate revocation lists (CRL), obtained by

trusted means from the same source that validates the authenticity of keys or certificates. Protected software that generates or regenerates keys or certificates may also be considered a cryptographic product.

SOURCE: CNSSI-4009

Cryptographic Randomization

Function that randomly determines the transmit state of a cryptographic logic.

SOURCE: CNSSI-4009

Cryptographic Security

Component of COMSEC resulting from the provision of technically sound cryptographic systems and their proper use.

SOURCE: CNSSI-4009

Cryptographic Strength

A measure of the expected number of operations required to defeat a cryptographic mechanism.

SOURCE: SP 800-63

Cryptographic Synchronization

Process by which a receiving decrypting cryptographic logic attains the same internal state as the transmitting encrypting logic.

SOURCE: CNSSI-4009

Cryptographic System

Associated information assurance items interacting to provide a single means of encryption or decryption.

SOURCE: CNSSI-4009

Cryptographic System Analysis

Process of establishing the exploitability of a cryptographic system, normally by reviewing transmitted traffic protected or secured by the system under study.

SOURCE: CNSSI-4009

Cryptographic System Evaluation

Process of determining vulnerabilities of a cryptographic system and recommending countermeasures.

SOURCE: CNSSI-4009

Cryptographic System Review	Examination of a cryptographic system by the controlling authority ensuring its adequacy of design and content, continued need, and proper distribution. SOURCE: CNSSI-4009
Cryptographic System Survey	Management technique in which actual holders of a cryptographic system express opinions on the system's suitability and provide usage information for technical evaluations. SOURCE: CNSSI-4009
Cryptographic Token	A token where the secret is a cryptographic key. SOURCE: SP 800-63
Cryptography	The discipline that embodies the principles, means, and methods for the transformation of data in order to hide its semantic content, prevent their unauthorized use, or prevent their undetected modification. SOURCE: SP 800-59
Data Encryption Algorithm (DEA)	The DEA cryptographic engine that is used by the Triple Data Encryption Algorithm (TDEA). SOURCE: SP 800-67
Data Encryption Standard (DES)	Cryptographic algorithm designed for the protection of unclassified data and published by the National Institute of Standards and Technology (NIST) in Federal Information Processing Standard (FIPS) Publication 46. (FIPS 46-3 withdrawn 19 May 2005) See Triple DES. SOURCE: CNSSI-4009
Data Flow Control	Synonymous with information flow control. SOURCE: CNSSI-4009

Decipher	Convert enciphered text to plaintext by means of a cryptographic system. SOURCE: CNSSI-4009
Decode	Convert encoded text to plaintext by means of a code. SOURCE: CNSSI-4009
Decrypt	Generic term encompassing decode and decipher. SOURCE: CNSSI-4009
Decryption	The process of transforming ciphertext into plaintext. SOURCE: SP 800-67
Digital Signature	An asymmetric key operation where the private key is used to digitally sign data and the public key is used to verify the signature. Digital signatures provide authenticity protection, integrity protection, and non-repudiation. SOURCE: SP 800-63
Digital Signature Algorithm	Asymmetric algorithms used for digitally signing data. SOURCE: SP 800-49
Electronic Key Entry	The entry of cryptographic keys into a cryptographic module using electronic methods such as a smart card or a key-loading device. (The operator of the key may have no knowledge of the value of the key being entered.) SOURCE: FIPS 140-2
Electronic Key Management System (EKMS)	Interoperable collection of systems being developed by services and agencies of the U.S. government to automate the planning, ordering, generating, distributing, storing, filling, using, and destroying of electronic key and management of other types of COMSEC material. SOURCE: CNSSI-4009

Embedded Cryptographic System	Cryptosystem performing or controlling a function as an integral element of a larger system or subsystem. Source: CNSSI-4009
Embedded Cryptography	Cryptography engineered into an equipment or system whose basic function is not cryptographic. Source: CNSSI-4009
Encipher	Convert plaintext to ciphertext by means of a cryptographic system. Source: CNSSI-4009
Encode	Convert plaintext to ciphertext by means of a code. Source: CNSSI-4009
Encrypt	Generic term encompassing encipher and encode. Source: CNSSI-4009
Encrypted Key	A cryptographic key that has been encrypted using an approved security function with a key encrypting key, a PIN, or a password in order to disguise the value of the underlying plaintext key. Source: FIPS 140-2
Encrypted Network	A network on which messages are encrypted (e.g., using DES, AES, or other appropriate algorithms) to prevent reading by unauthorized parties. Source: SP 800-32
Encryption	Conversion of plaintext to ciphertext through the use of a cryptographic algorithm. Source: FIPS 185
Encryption Algorithm	Set of mathematically expressed rules for rendering data unintelligible by executing a series of conversions controlled by a key. Source: CNSSI-4009

Encryption Certificate	A certificate containing a public key that is used to encrypt electronic messages, files, documents, or data transmissions, or to establish or exchange a session key for these same purposes. SOURCE: SP 800-32
End-to-End Encryption	Communications encryption in which data is encrypted when being passed through a network, but routing information remains visible. SOURCE: SP 800-12
Federal Public Key Infrastructure Policy Authority (FPKI PA)	The Federal PKI Policy Authority is a federal government body responsible for setting, implementing, and administering policy decisions regarding interagency PKI inter-operability that uses the FBCA. SOURCE: SP 800-32
File Encryption	The process of encrypting individual files on a storage medium and permitting access to the encrypted data only after proper authentication is provided. SOURCE: SP 800-111
FIPS-Approved Security Method	A security method (e.g., cryptographic algorithm, cryptographic key generation algorithm or key distribution technique, random number generator, authentication technique, or evaluation criteria) that is either a) specified in a FIPS or b) adopted in a FIPS. SOURCE: FIPS 196
FIPS-Validated Cryptography	A cryptographic module validated by the Cryptographic Module Validation Program (CMVP) to meet requirements specified in FIPS 140-2 (as amended). As a prerequisite to CMVP validation, the cryptographic module is required to employ a cryptographic

algorithm implementation that has successfully passed validation testing by the Cryptographic Algorithm Validation Program
(CAVP). See NSA-Approved Cryptography.

SOURCE: SP 800-53

FIPS PUB

An acronym for Federal Information Processing Standards Publication. FIPS publications (PUB) are issued by NIST after
approval by the Secretary of Commerce.

SOURCE: SP 800-64

Forward Cipher

One of the two functions of the block cipher
algorithm that is determined by the choice of
a cryptographic key. The term "forward cipher
operation" is used for TDEA, while the term
"forward transformation" is used for DEA.

SOURCE: SP 800-67

Full Disk Encryption (FDE)

The process of encrypting all the data on the
hard disk drive used to boot a computer,
including the computer's operating system,
and permitting access to the data only after
successful authentication with the full disk
encryption product.

SOURCE: SP 800-111

Hash Function

A function that maps a bit string of arbitrary length to a fixed-length bit string.
Approved hash functions satisfy the
following properties:

1) One-Way. It is computationally infeasible
   to find any input that maps to any
   prespecified output.

2) Collision Resistant. It is computationally
   infeasible to find any two distinct inputs
   that map to the same output.

SOURCE: SP 800-63; FIPS 201

Hash Value	The result of applying a cryptographic hash function to data (e.g., a message).
	SOURCE: SP 800-106
Hash-based Message Authentication Code (HMAC)	A message authentication code that uses a cryptographic key in conjunction with a hash function.
	SOURCE: FIPS 201; CNSSI-4009
Hashing	The process of using a mathematical algorithm against data to produce a numeric value that is representative of that data.
	SOURCE: SP 800-72; CNSSI-4009
Integrity	Guarding against improper information modification or destruction, and includes ensuring information nonrepudiation and authenticity.
	SOURCE: SP 800-53; SP 800-53A; SP 800-18; SP 800-27; SP 800-37; SP 800-60; FIPS 200; FIPS 199; 44 U.S.C., Sec. 3542
Internet Protocol (IP)	Standard protocol for transmission of data from source to destinations in packet-switched communications networks and interconnected systems of such networks.
	SOURCE: CNSSI-4009
Key	A value used to control cryptographic operations, such as decryption, encryption, signature generation, or signature verification.
	SOURCE: SP 800-63
Key Bundle	The three cryptographic keys (Key1, Key2, Key3) that are used with a Triple Data Encryption Algorithm (TDEA) mode.
	SOURCE: SP 800-67
Key Distribution Center (KDC)	COMSEC facility generating and distributing key in electronic form.
	SOURCE: CNSSI-4009

Key Escrow	A deposit of the private key of a subscriber and other pertinent information pursuant to an escrow agreement or similar contract binding upon the subscriber, the terms of which require one or more agents to hold the subscriber's private key for the benefit of the subscriber, an employer, or other party, upon provisions set forth in the agreement.

SOURCE: SP 800-32

The processes of managing (e.g., generating, storing, transferring, auditing) the two components of a cryptographic key by two key component holders.

SOURCE: FIPS 185

1. The processes of managing (e.g., generating, storing, transferring, auditing) the two components of a cryptographic key by two key component holders.

2. A key recovery technique for storing knowledge of a cryptographic key, or parts thereof, in the custody of one or more third parties called "escrow agents," so that the key can be recovered and used in specified circumstances.

SOURCE: CNSSI-4009

Key Escrow System	A system that entrusts the two components comprising a cryptographic key (e.g., a device unique key) to two key component holders (also called "escrow agents").

SOURCE: FIPS 185; CNSSI-4009

Key Establishment	The process by which cryptographic keys are securely established among cryptographic modules using manual transport methods (e.g., key loaders), automated methods (e.g., key transport and/or key agreement

protocols), or a combination of automated and manual methods (consists of key transport plus key agreement).

SOURCE: FIPS 140-2

The process by which cryptographic keys are securely established among cryptographic modules using key transport and/ or key agreement procedures. See Key Distribution.

SOURCE: CNSSI-4009

Key Exchange

The process of exchanging public keys in order to establish secure communications.

SOURCE: SP 800-32

Process of exchanging public keys (and other information) in order to establish secure communications.

SOURCE: CNSSI-4009

Key Expansion

Routine used to generate a series of Round Keys from the Cipher Key.

SOURCE: FIPS 197

Key Generation Material

Random numbers, pseudo-random numbers, and cryptographic parameters used in generating cryptographic keys.

SOURCE: SP 800-32; CNSSI-4009

Key List

Printed series of key settings for a specific cryptonet. Key lists may be produced in list, pad, or printed tape format.

SOURCE: CNSSI-4009

Key Loader

A self-contained unit that is capable of storing at least one plaintext or encrypted cryptographic key or key component that can be transferred, upon request, into a cryptographic module.

SOURCE: FIPS 140-2

Key Management	The activities involving the handling of cryptographic keys and other related security parameters (e.g., IVs and passwords) during the entire life cycle of the keys, including their generation, storage, establishment, entry and output, and zeroization. SOURCE: FIPS 140-2; CNSSI-4009
Key Management Device	A unit that provides for secure electronic distribution of encryption keys to authorized users. SOURCE: CNSSI-4009
Key Management Infrastructure—(KMI)	All parts—computer hardware, firmware, software, and other equipment and its documentation; facilities that house the equipment and related functions; and companion standards, policies, procedures, and doctrine that form the system that manages and supports the ordering and delivery of cryptographic material and related information products and services to users. SOURCE: CNSSI-4009
Key Pair	Two mathematically related keys having the properties that (1) one key can be used to encrypt a message that can only be decrypted using the other key and (2) even knowing one key, it is computationally infeasible to discover the other key. SOURCE: SP 800-32 A public key and its corresponding private key; a key pair is used with a public key algorithm. SOURCE: SP 800-21; CNSSI-4009
Key Production Key (KPK)	Key used to initialize a keystream generator for the production of other electronically generated key. SOURCE: CNSSI-4009

Key Recovery	Mechanisms and processes that allow authorized parties to retrieve the cryptographic key used for data confidentiality. SOURCE: CNSSI-4009
Key Stream	Sequence of symbols (or their electrical or mechanical equivalents) produced in a machine or auto-manual cryptosystem to combine with plaintext to produce ciphertext, control transmission security processes, or produce key. SOURCE: CNSSI-4009
Link Encryption	Link encryption encrypts all of the data along a communications path (e.g., a satellite link, telephone circuit, or T1 line). Since link encryption also encrypts routing data, communications nodes need to decrypt the data to continue routing. SOURCE: SP 800-12
Manual Cryptosystem	Cryptosystem in which the cryptographic processes are performed without the use of crypto-equipment or auto-manual devices. SOURCE: CNSSI-4009
Message Authentication Code—(MAC)	A cryptographic checksum on data that uses a symmetric key to detect both accidental and intentional modifications of the data. MACs provide authenticity and integrity protection, but not non-repudiation protection. SOURCE: SP 800-63; FIPS 201
Minimalist Cryptography	Cryptography that can be implemented on devices with very limited memory and computing capabilities, such as RFID tags. SOURCE: SP 800-98
Nondeterministic Random Bit Generator (NRBG)	An RBG that (when working properly) produces outputs that have full entropy. Contrast with a DRBG. Other names for

nondeterministic RBGs are True Random Number (or Bit) Generators and, simply, Random Number (or Bit) Generators.

SOURCE: SP 800-90A

NSA-Approved Cryptography	Cryptography that consists of: (1) an approved algorithm; (2) an implementation that has been approved for the protection of classified information in a particular environment; and (3) a supporting key management infrastructure.

SOURCE: SP 800-53

Offline Cryptosystem   Cryptographic system in which encryption and decryption are performed independently of the transmission and reception functions.

SOURCE: CNSSI-4009

Over-the-Air Key Distribution   Providing electronic key via over-the-air rekeying, over-the-air key transfer, or cooperative key generation.

SOURCE: CNSSI-4009

Over-the-Air Key Transfer   Electronically distributing key without changing traffic encryption key used on the secured communications path over which the transfer is accomplished.

SOURCE: CNSSI-4009

Over-the-Air Rekeying (OTAR)   Changing traffic encryption key or transmission security key in remote cryptographic equipment by sending new key directly to the remote cryptographic equipment over the communications path it secures.

SOURCE: CNSSI-4009

Plaintext Key   An unencrypted cryptographic key.

SOURCE: FIPS 140-2

Private Key   The secret part of an asymmetric key pair that is typically used to digitally sign or decrypt data.

SOURCE: SP 800-63

A cryptographic key, used with a public key cryptographic algorithm, that is uniquely associated with an entity and is not made public. In an asymmetric (public) cryptosystem, the private key is associated with a public key. Depending on the algorithm, the private key may be used, for example, to:

1) compute the corresponding public key,

2) compute a digital signature that may be verified by the corresponding public key,

3) decrypt keys that were encrypted by the corresponding public key, or

4) compute a shared secret during a key-agreement transaction.

SOURCE: SP 800-57 Part 1

Public Key

The public part of an asymmetric key pair that is typically used to verify signatures or encrypt data.

SOURCE: FIPS 201; SP 800-63

Public Key Certificate

A digital document issued and digitally signed by the private key of a certificate authority that binds the name of a subscriber to a public key. The certificate indicates that the subscriber identified in the certificate has sole control and access to the private key.

SOURCE: SP 800-63

Public Key (Asymmetric) Cryptographic Algorithm

A cryptographic algorithm that uses two related keys, a public key and a private key. The two keys have the property that deriving the private key from the public key is computationally infeasible.

SOURCE: FIPS 140-2

Public Key Cryptography

Encryption system that uses a public-private key pair for encryption and/or digital signature.

SOURCE: CNSSI-4009

Public Key Enabling (PKE)	The incorporation of the use of certificates for security services such as authentication, confidentiality, data integrity, and non-repudiation. SOURCE: CNSSI-4009
Public Key Infrastructure (PKI)	A set of policies, processes, server platforms, software, and workstations used for the purpose of administering certificates and public-private key pairs, including the ability to issue, maintain, and revoke public key certificates. SOURCE: SP 800-32; SP 800-63
Rekey	To change the value of a cryptographic key that is being used in a cryptographic system/application. SOURCE: CNSSI-4009
Rekey (a certificate)	To change the value of a cryptographic key that is being used in a cryptographic system application; this normally entails issuing a new certificate on the new public key. SOURCE: SP 800-32
Rijndael	Cryptographic algorithm specified in the Advanced Encryption Standard (AES). SOURCE: FIPS 197
Root Certification Authority	In a hierarchical Public Key Infrastructure, the Certification Authority whose public key serves as the most trusted datum (i.e., the beginning of trust paths) for a security domain. SOURCE: SP 800-32; CNSSI-4009
Salt	A non-secret value that is used in a cryptographic process, usually to ensure that the results of computations for one instance cannot be reused by an attacker. SOURCE: SP 800-63; CNSSI-4009

Secret Key (symmetric) Cryptographic Algorithm	A cryptographic algorithm that uses a single secret key for both encryption and decryption.
	SOURCE: FIPS 140-2
	A cryptographic algorithm that uses a single key (i.e., a secret key) for both encryption and decryption.
	SOURCE: CNSSI-4009
Secret Seed	A secret value used to initialize a pseudo-random number generator.
	SOURCE: CNSSI-4009
Secure/Multipurpose Internet Mail Extensions (S/MIME)	A set of specifications for securing electronic mail. S/MIME is based upon the widely used MIME standard [MIME] and describes a protocol for adding cryptographic security services through MIME encapsulation of digitally signed and encrypted objects. The basic security services offered by S/MIME are authentication, nonrepudiation of origin, message integrity, and message privacy.
	Optional security services include signed receipts, security labels, secure mailing lists, and an extended method of identifying the signer's certificate(s).
	SOURCE: SP 800-49; CNSSI-4009
Secure Socket Layer (SSL)	A protocol used for protecting private information during transmission via the Internet.
	Note: SSL works by using a public key to encrypt data that's transferred over the SSL connection. Most Web browsers support SSL, and many Web sites use the protocol to obtain confidential user information, such as credit card numbers. By convention, URLs that require an SSL connection start with "https:" instead of "http:."
	SOURCE: CNSSI-4009

Signed Data

Data on which a digital signature is generated.

SOURCE: FIPS 196

Static Key

A key that is intended for use for a relatively long period of time and is typically intended for use in many instances of a cryptographic key establish scheme.

SOURCE: SP 800-57 Part 1

Subordinate Certification Authority

In a hierarchical PKI, a Certification Authority whose certificate signature key is certified by another CA, and whose activities are constrained by that other CA.

SOURCE: SP 800-32; CNSSI-4009

Symmetric Encryption Algorithm

Encryption algorithms using the same secret key for encryption and decryption.

SOURCE: SP 800-49; CNSSI-4009

Symmetric Key

A cryptographic key that is used to perform both the cryptographic operation and its inverse, for example to encrypt and decrypt, or create a message authentication code and to verify the code.

SOURCE: SP 800-63; CNSSI-4009

Token

Something that the claimant possesses and controls (typically a key or password) that is used to authenticate the claimant's identity.

SOURCE: SP 800-63

Traffic Encryption Key (TEK)

Key used to encrypt plaintext or to super-encrypt previously encrypted text and/or to decrypt ciphertext.

SOURCE: CNSSI-4009

Transport Layer Security (TLS)

An authentication and security protocol widely implemented in browsers and Web servers.

SOURCE: SP 800-63

Trusted Agent	Entity authorized to act as a representative of an agency in confirming subscriber identification during the registration process. Trusted Agents do not have automated interfaces with Certification Authorities.
	SOURCE: SP 800-32; CNSSI-4009
Trusted Certificate	A certificate that is trusted by the Relying Party on the basis of secure and authenticated delivery. The public keys included in trusted certificates are used to start certification paths. Also known as a "trust anchor."
	SOURCE: SP 800-32; CNSSI-4009
Trusted Channel	A channel where the endpoints are known and data integrity is protected in transit. Depending on the communications protocol used, data privacy may be protected in transit. Examples include SSL, IPSEC, and secure physical connection.
	SOURCE: CNSSI-4009
Trusted Computer System	A system that employs sufficient hardware and software assurance measures to allow its use for processing simultaneously a range of sensitive or classified information.
	SOURCE: CNSSI-4009
Trusted Computing Base (TCB)	Totality of protection mechanisms within a computer system, including hardware, firmware, and software, the combination responsible for enforcing a security policy.
	SOURCE: CNSSI-4009
	A means by which an operator and a target of evaluation security function can communicate with the necessary confidence to support the target of evaluation security policy.
	SOURCE: FIPS 140-2

Trusted Platform Module (TPM) Chip	A tamper-resistant integrated circuit built into some computer motherboards that can perform cryptographic operations (including key generation) and protect small amounts of sensitive information, such as passwords and cryptographic keys. SOURCE: SP 800-111
Wi-Fi Protected Access-2 (WPA2)	The approved Wi-Fi Alliance interoperable Timplementation of the IEEE 802.11i security standard. For federal government use, the implementation must use FIPS-approved encryption, such as AES. SOURCE: CNSSI-4009
Wired Equivalent Privacy (WEP)	A security protocol, specified in the IEEE 802.11 standard, that is designed to provide a WLAN with a level of security and privacy comparable to what is usually expected of a wired LAN. WEP is no longer considered a viable encryption mechanism due to known weaknesses. SOURCE: SP 800-48
Wireless Access Point (WAP)	A device that acts as a conduit to connect wireless communication devices together to allow them to communicate and create a wireless network. SOURCE: CNSSI-4009
X.509 Public Key Certificate	A digital certificate containing a public key for entity and a name for the entity, together with some other information that is rendered unforgeable by the digital signature of the certification authority that issued the certificate, encoded in the format defined in the ISO/ITU-T SOURCE: SP 800-57 Part 1; CNSSI-4009 adapted

Index

The Lawyer's Guide to Microsoft® Word 2013
By Ben M. Schorr

Product Code: 5110757 • LP Price: $41.95 • Regular Price: $69.95

Microsoft® Word is one of the most used applications in the Microsoft® Office suite. This handy reference includes clear explanations, legal-specific descriptions, and time-saving tips for getting the most out of Microsoft Word®--and customizing it for the needs of today's legal professional. Focusing on the tools and features that are essential for lawyers in their everyday practice, *The Lawyer's Guide to Microsoft® Word 2013* explains in detail the key components to help make you more effective, more efficient, and more successful. Written specifically for lawyers by a twenty-year veteran of legal technology, this guide will introduce you to Microsoft® Word 2013.

Legal Project Management in One Hour for Lawyers
By Pamela H. Woldow and Douglas B. Richardson

Product Code: 5110763 • LP Price: $39.95 • Regular Price: $49.95

Legal clients are responding to today's unprecedented financial pressures by demanding better predictability, cost-effectiveness and communication from their outside legal service providers. They give their business to those who can manage legal work efficiently--and take it away from those who can't or won't. *Legal Project Management in One Hour for Lawyers* provides any attorney with practical skills and methods for improving efficiency, keeping budgets under control, building strong working relationships with clients, and maximizing profitability.

Adobe Acrobat in One Hour for Lawyers
By Ernie Svenson

Product Code: 5110768 • LP Price: $39.95 • Regular Price: $49.95

Most lawyers now encounter PDFs, and many own Adobe Acrobat--the most widely used software for working with PDFs. But most attorneys are confused about how to work efficiently with PDFs. *Adobe Acrobat in One Hour for Lawyers* is written for lawyers and legal professionals who want to be more organized by making better use of PDFs.

Quickbooks in One Hour for Lawyers
By Lynette Benton

Product Code: 5110764 • LP Price: $39.95 • Regular Price: $49.95

Spend more time practicing law--and less time balancing the books--by investing in easy and effective accounting software. Lynette Benton, a QuickBooks certified ProAdvisor and consultant who has helped hundreds of attorneys and small firms with financial management, will teach you to use this popular accounting software in your law practice. *QuickBooks in One Hour for Lawyers* offers step-by-step guidance for getting started with QuickBooks and putting it to work tracking income, expenses, time, billing, and much more.

WordPress in One Hour for Lawyers: How to Create a Website for Your Law Firm
By Jennifer Ellis

Product Code: 5110767 • LP Price: $39.95 • Regular Price: $49.95

Law firms without websites are placing themselves at a great disadvantage compared with the competition. Even if you feel you receive the majority of your clients through referrals, a website provides the opportunity for those potential clients to learn about you and your firm. This book will explain how to get create your firm's website quickly and easily with WordPress®software.

Twitter in One Hour for Lawyers
By Jared Correia

Product Code: 5110746 • LP Price: $24.95 • Regular Price: $39.95

More lawyers than ever before are using Twitter to network with colleagues, attract clients, market their law firms, and even read the news. But to the uninitiated, Twitter's short messages, or tweets, can seem like they are written in a foreign language. *Twitter in One Hour for Lawyers* will demystify one of the most important social-media platforms of our time and teach you to tweet like an expert.

Virtual Law Practice: How to Deliver Legal Services Online
By Stephanie L. Kimbro

Product Code: 5110707 • LP Price: $47.95 • Regular Price: $79.95

The legal market has recently experienced a dramatic shift as lawyers seek out alternative methods of practicing law and providing more affordable legal services. Virtual law practice is revolutionizing the way the public receives legal services and how legal professionals work with clients.

Worldox in One Hour for Lawyers
By John Heckman

Product Code: 5110771 • LP Price: $39.95 • Regular Price: $49.95

Never lose another document or waste valuable time searching for one. In just one hour, learn how to organize your documents and e-mails electronically with Worldox software. Veteran law-firm technology consult John Heckman reveals what Worldox will do for your firm--and how to customize its features for the specific needs of your practice.

PowerPoint in One Hour for Lawyers
By John Heckman

Product Code: 5110771 • LP Price: $39.95 • Regular Price: $49.95

The difference between a successful presentation and an unsuccessful one can often be traced to a presenter's use--or misuse--of PowerPoint®. *PowerPoint in One Hour for Lawyers* offers practical advice for creating effective presentations quickly and easily. PowerPoint expert and attorney Paul Unger will help you avoid mishaps and develop a compelling presentation using storyboarding techniques.

30-DAY RISK-FREE ORDER FORM

ABA**LAW**
PRACTICE
DIVISION
The Business of Practicing Law

Please print or type. To ship UPS, we must have your street address. If you list a P.O. Box, we will ship by U.S. Mail.

Name

Member ID

Firm/Organization

Street Address

City/State/Zip

Area Code/Phone (In case we have a question about your order)

E-mail

Method of Payment:
☐ Check enclosed, payable to American Bar Association
☐ MasterCard   ☐ Visa   ☐ American Express

Card Number   Expiration Date

Signature Required

MAIL THIS FORM TO:
American Bar Association, Publication Orders
P.O. Box 10892, Chicago, IL 60610

ORDER BY PHONE:
24 hours a day, 7 days a week:
Call 1-800-285-2221 to place a credit card order. We accept Visa, MasterCard, and American Express.

EMAIL ORDERS: orders@americanbar.org
FAX ORDERS: 1-312-988-5568

VISIT OUR WEB SITE: www.ShopABA.org
Allow 7-10 days for regular UPS delivery. Need it sooner? Ask about our overnight delivery options. Call the ABA Service Center at 1-800-285-2221 for more information.

GUARANTEE:
If–for any reason–you are not satisfied with your purchase, you may return it within 30 days of receipt for a refund of the price of the book(s). No questions asked.

Thank You For Your Order.

Join the ABA Law Practice Division today and receive a substantial discount on Division publications!

Product Code:	Description:	Quantity:	Price:	Total Price:
				$
				$
				$
				$
				$

Shipping/Handling:		*Tax:	Subtotal:	$
$0.00 to $9.99	add $0.00	IL residents add 9.25% DC residents add 5.75%	*Tax:	$
$10.00 to $49.99	add $6.95			
$50.00 to $99.99	add $8.95		**Shipping/Handling:	$
$100.00 to $199.99	add $10.95	Yes, I am an ABA member and would like to join the Law Practice Division today! (Add $50.00)		$
$200.00 to $499.99	add $13.95		Total:	$